Sweet & Simple
COUNTRY
QUILTS

Sweet & Simple
COUNTRY QUILTS

Jenni Dobson

with quilt designs by Anny Evason

Illustrations by Penny Brown

Sterling Publishing Co., Inc. New York

A STERLING / MUSEUM QUILTS BOOK

ACKNOWLEDGEMENTS

Many thanks are due to Mission Valley Textiles, Inc. for supplying the wonderful plaids and stripes, Shirley Simpson for the hand-dyed fabrics and Strawberry Fayre for supplying the backing, wadding and plain fabrics. Also to the following project makers:
Pat Allen, Jennifer Almond, Peggy Bell, Colin Brandi, Bryonny Burdell,
Sharon Cockerill, Carol Dennis, Judith Gill, Angela Guppy, Yvonne Holland, Linda Maltman,
Mary Mayne, Irene Nowell, Patricia Payn, Anne Perrin, Gaynor Sandercock,
Veronika Smith, Lyn Spencer, Margaret Torrance and June Walters whose talents and efforts turned our designs into reality.

A STERLING/MUSEUM QUILTS BOOK

Library of Congress
Cataloging-in-Publication Data Available

2 4 6 8 10 9 7 5 3 1

Published by Sterling Publishing Company, Inc., 387 Park Avenue South, New York, NY 10016
Published in the UK by Museum Quilts (UK) Inc., 254-258 Goswell Road, London EC1V 7EB
Distributed in Canada by Sterling Publishing c/o Canadian Manda Group,
One Atlantic Avenue, Suite 105, Toronto, Ontario, Canada M6K 3E7
Distributed in Australia by Capricorn Link (Australia) Pty Ltd., P.O.
Box 6651, Baulkham Hills Business Centre NSW 2153, Australia

Copyright © Museum Quilts Publications, Inc. 1996

Text © Jenni Dobson 1996
Illustrations © Penny Brown 1996

Editor: Ljiljana Ortolja-Baird
Designer: Kit Johnson

ISBN: 0-8069-9497-5

Printed and bound in Spain

Contents

Foreword

We commissioned artist Anny Evason to dream up a series of "sweet and simple country quilts" that would satisfy the enormous interest currently being expressed by quilters for new folk and country designs that are worked in plaids, checks and stripes. Her brief was to come up with a variety of designs that would include large and simple piecing and appliqué motifs that would encourage newcomers to quilting while remaining a challenge to experienced quilters.

Based on an imaginary country community, and inspired by a number of different folk art styles, Anny has created in her collection of quilt projects an amusing picture gallery of country folk and their activities. There is the robust Swineherd and her companion the Shepherd; the spirited hoe-down Dancing Couples and the hard-working Ploughman; the determined Goosegirl and lively Cowboy. Each character has a story to tell, and each design is a charming and often witty evocation of the perfect rural life.

Quilter and author Jenni Dobson has had the task of realizing Anny's designs into "real" quilts. Translating flat artwork into a functional, three-dimensional piece of needlecraft takes considerable skill, especially if the designs do not conform to conventional quilting practices.

Jenni has made the quilts and projects using the most up-to-date, economical and speedy sewing methods, and wherever possible she encourages readers to find their own sewing solutions and fabric choices that best suit their skills and preferences.

There are sixteen main quilt and wallhanging designs and a number of smaller associated projects that use motifs from the main designs. Each quilt features one or more of the characters in the activity of their labor. The Cowboy rounds up the cattle, the Chickengirl rescues a hen from a snatching fox, the Old Homestead Couple churns the butter and the Goosegirl marches the geese to market. The projects culminate in a magnificent Marriage quilt in which all the characters appear in procession as guests of

the wedding couple who occupy the central medallion.

The projects in this book were made with fabrics generously donated by Mission Valley Textiles in Texas. Most fabric suppliers now carry a good range of Mission Valley fabrics; however, if these fabrics are not readily to hand there are many other textile companies offering a wide selection of alternative homespun plaids and checks. Besides, there is absolutely no need to adhere to our fabric choices. The "sweet and simple" quilts follow in the great tradition of scrap quilts, so if you don't have a particular fabric or run out, find a substitute from among the fabrics that you do have.

I hope you'll enjoy this "sweet and simple" country where fabric meets fiction.

The Old Homestead Quilt

This double quilt boasts many features commonly associated with Folk Art quilts. There are

pictorial blocks, pieced blocks, decorative filler blocks with appliqué leaves,

flowers, hearts, stars and moons, all fitted together with simple strip piecing. Although the

design of the quilt may appear complicated, rest assured that you can approach

it in a relaxed manner, building up each component as you go along.

SIZE $83 \times 82\frac{1}{2}$ in / 210.8×209.6 cm

MATERIALS

● Yardage requirements for the plaid fabrics only are based on 60 in/ 150 cm wide Mission Valley fabrics.

$2\frac{1}{2}$ yd × 90 in wide/2.3 m × 228.6 cm wide calico for backing

1 Queen size wadding

$1\frac{1}{2}$ yd/1.4 m dark plaid for border

$\frac{3}{4}$ yd/0.7m red plaid for binding

2 yd/2 m pale plaid for Churning Couple and Milkmaid block backgrounds

$\frac{1}{2}$ yd/0.5 m black and white plaid for homestead background, cows and corners of pieced blocks

Scraps of gold print, bold plaid, pale plaid or plain, plus black for the homestead

$\frac{1}{2}$ yd/0.5 m black for trees, windmill, churns etc.

$\frac{3}{4}$ yd/0.7 m beige for faces, hands and appliqué block backgrounds

Assorted rectangles of plains and plaids for remaining appliqué block backgrounds

Scraps of red, wine, rust, pale yellow, grey, pink for figurative blocks

$\frac{1}{4}$ yd/0.25 m each of two small green plaids for oak leaves and the strip piecing

18×6 in/45.7 × 15.2 cm violet for border patch and confetti spots

Scraps of blue-grey for bird, brown, cinnamon, gold, geranium pink and other bright plains for flowers and confetti spots

Scraps of greys, greens, blues, yellows, peach, beige, tan for pieced blocks

Mixed plaid scraps equivalent to 1 yd/ 1 m for the strip-pieced filler blocks

PATTERNS

This quilt was worked using the freezer paper method, so for each appliqué piece the shape was traced in reverse on the paper side of the freezer paper. When cut out, these papers are used as templates for cutting the fabric shapes. Make one tracing for each time the shape appears, making sure to make the necessary reversals for the required blocks. No patterns have been provided for the confetti spots. These can be cut freehand. Leaves and flowers can be cut freehand.

Draft the 10 in/25.4 cm pieced block based on a 2 in/5 cm square unit. Make templates from this full-size pattern or follow step 8 of the cutting instructions to strip-cut without templates.

CUTTING

1. Cut six strips 4½ in/11.5 cm deep across the full width of the plaid border fabric. For the border patch, cut a strip of violet 12½ × 4½ in/31.7 × 11.5 cm.

2. Cut six strips 2½ in/6.5 cm deep across the full width of the red plaid for the binding.

3. From the pale plaid background fabric, cut three squares 22 × 22 in/ 56 × 56 cm for the Churning Couple blocks 1–3. Cut two rectangles 26 × 21 in/66 × 53.3 cm for the Milkmaid blocks 4–5.

4. From the black and white plaid cut a rectangle 18 × 11 in/45.7 × 28 cm for the homestead block.

5. Using the illustration on page 11 as a guide, cut block backgrounds for the remaining appliqué blocks as follows:

Block no.	
7	16 × 13½ in/40.7 × 34.3 cm
8	13½ × 13 in/34.3 × 33 cm
9	16½ × 13 in/42 × 33 cm
10	9¼ × 18¼ in/23.5 × 46.5 cm
11	8¼ × 17½ in/21 × 44.5 cm
12	5 × 9 in/12.7 × 23 cm
13	22 × 5 in/56 × 12.7 cm
14	8½ × 8 in/21.5 × 20.3 cm
15	9½ × 9¾ in/24 × 24.8 cm
16	8½ × 8½ in/21.5 × 21.5 cm
17	8¾ × 8¾ in/22.2 × 22.2 cm
18	6¾ × 9¾ in/17.2 × 24.8 cm
19	8½ × 9¼ in/21.5 × 23.5 cm
20	9 × 8 in/23 × 20.3 cm
21	10 × 8 in/25.5 × 20.3 cm
22	8¾ × 8½ in/22.2 × 21.5 cm
23	8½ × 8¾ in/21.5 × 22.2 cm
24	8½ × 8¼ in/21.5 × 21 cm
25	9½ × 8¼ in/24 × 21 cm
26	8¾ × 8 in/22.2 × 20.3 cm

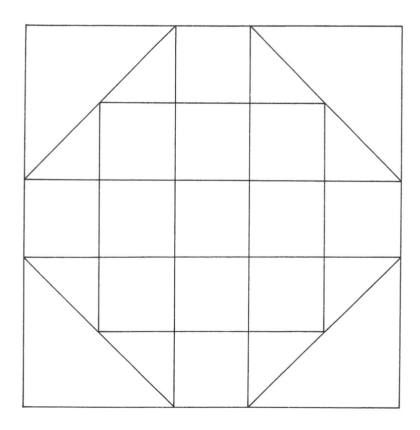

required. When cutting remember to add ½ in/1.3 cm seam allowance to the required finished width of the strip. Notice that not all the strips in a block are the same width.

SEWING

1. Appliqué the large blocks first, then the smaller ones. Small component pieces like the strips on the barrel, hatbands, flower and windmill centers can be appliquéd in position before the complete motif is sewn to the block.

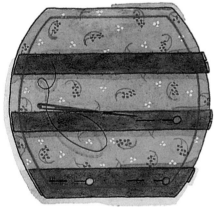

6. Using the freezer paper templates, ironed waxy-side to the WS of the fabric, and adding ¼ in/0.6 cm in turnings by eye as you go, cut the appliqué pieces for the figures in the picture blocks and the motifs in the smaller blocks. Do not remove the freezer paper shapes.

7. To avoid sewing narrow strips for the window and door frames cut a square or rectangle, adding ¼ in/0.6 cm turning, from a pale colored fabric. Appliqué a smaller shape of black on top.

8. Following the photograph for color placement, cut the pieces for the pieced blocks. To strip-cut the squares, cut strips 2½ in/6.4 cm wide and cross-cut into squares. For the small triangles, cut squares 2⅞ × 2⅞ in/7.3 × 7.3 cm in half diagonally. For the large corner triangles, cut squares 4⅞ × 4⅞ in/12.4 × 12.4 cm in half diagonally.

9. You will need strips for the filler blocks but these should be cut after the blocks have been worked so you can check the exact measurements

To ensure all parts of the block pictures fit together correctly, the turnings can be tacked over the ironed-on freezer paper shapes. Do not turn under any edges which will be overlapped by neighboring shapes. Secure the underneath parts with a little running stitch, leaving a small gap to ease out the freezer paper before placing on the next piece. If you forget to leave a gap, or for shapes that are completely enclosed, slit the background fabric carefully to remove the paper.

2. Make the narrow window and door frames as described in Cutting, step 7 above.

3. The bird on block 14 overlaps block 11. Don't finish sewing the bird to the block until the two blocks have been sewn together.

4. After sewing, press each block face down over a thick towel, then trim to size given on the quilt plan. The measurements include ¼ in/ 0.6 cm on all sides. Should any of your blocks seem too small, simply add a strip to the appropriate edge to bring it to size.

5. Make the six pieced blocks.

6. When all the blocks are finished, lay them out according to the plan; or you may consider a completely different arrangement to the one shown. Measure them to work out the sizes needed for the strip-pieced filler blocks. Remember to add seam allowances when cutting.

7. Strip-piece the filler blocks, press and trim to fit. Assemble the units together as you go. This makes it easier to calculate the dimensions for the blocks still to be made. The plan suggests a suitable way to group the units together but because some of the units do not fit together in neat rows, some seams will require insetting. One way to deal with this is to press under ¼ in/0.6 cm turning on the edge of one unit, overlap this ¼ in/0.6 cm over the appropriate pieces and sew in place as for appliqué.

Alternatively, sew the seams in two stages. Carefully mark the corner points on both pieces. Match these points on one side of the corner and sew this part of the seam.

Then fold the fabric to line up with the remaining edges and sew the second part. Consistent and accurate seam allowances are essential to successful insetting.

side borders. Divide two of the full width strips cut earlier into half and join one each of these to the remaining four strips, including the violet patch in one strip. Mark the required length for the side borders on two of these strips. Do not trim. Press, then measure the width of the quilt. Mark this on the remaining borders and sew them to the top and bottom of the quilt, trimming the excess afterwards.

8. When all the parts are assembled, measure the length of the quilt through the center for the

9. Press the quilt top and backing carefully. Spread the backing, RS down, and the wadding on a flat surface, then center the top, RS up, over them. Pin and tack the layers together. Quilt around the appliqué shapes and around each block, about ⅛ in/0.3 cm from all seams.

10. Join the binding strips to make a continuous length and bind the quilt to finish, following the directions in the General Techniques chapter.

Tote Bags

These two all-purpose bags are an ideal solution when you are looking for quick and easy gifts
to make. The center panels can contain any motif from the book or a design of your
own choice, and the pieced panel surrounds offer opportunities to use up your fabric scraps.

Bird and Oakleaf Tote Bag

The large bag features the skittish bird from the Old Homestead quilt as

the central panel. It is surrounded by a dramatic sawtooth border, small appliqué oak leaf

blocks and a variety of patchwork shapes.

SIZE 17 × 14 in / 43 × 35.5 cm

MATERIALS

Lining: two pieces each 17½ × 14½ in / 44.5 × 36.8 cm

Wadding: two pieces each 17½ × 14½ in / 44.5 × 36.8 cm, two pieces each 19½ × 1 in / 49.5 × 2.5 cm for handles, one piece 6 × 4½ in / 15.2 × 11.5 cm for tab

Red, black and beige plaid: one piece 17½ × 14½ in / 44.5 × 36.8 cm for bag back, two pieces each 19½ × 3¼ in / 49.5 × 8.3 cm for handles, two pieces 6 × 4½ in / 15.2 × 11.5 cm for tab plus strips for piecing

Red and beige plaid: 29½ × 2 in / 75 × 5 cm to bind top edge

Beige and black plaid: one square 4½ × 4½ in / 11.5 × 11.5 cm for central appliqué block

Two different plaids: one rectangle 12 × 6 in / 30.5 × 15.2 cm of each

Assorted scraps for piecing and appliqué

Embroidery thread for details

PATTERNS

Make templates from the Old Homestead quilt of the skittish bird to measure 3½ in / 9 cm high and the oak leaf to measure 1½ in / 4 cm. Make a paper pattern for the tab.

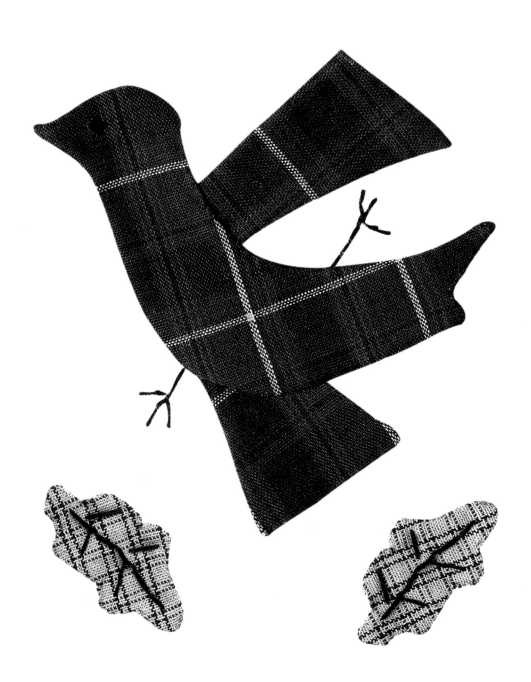

CUTTING

1. Cut out the bag pieces as listed under Materials.

2. From your scrap bag cut six squares each 2½ × 2½ in / 6.4 × 6.4 cm for the appliqué block background. Also cut a few strips 2½ in / 6.4 cm wide and no longer than 8½ in / 21.5 cm for setting the appliqué blocks.

3. Trace around the appliqué templates and cut out the bird and six oak leaves.

SEWING

1. Appliqué the bird onto the 4½ in / 11.5 cm square.

2. Embroider his eye and legs.

3. Appliqué the oak leaves to the 2½ in / 6.4 cm squares. To keep the appliqué motifs away from the edges, trim slightly in one direction to conform with neighboring shapes. Embroider the leaf veins.

4. Using the two 12 × 6 in / 30.5 × 15.2 cm rectangles mark out a grid of eight squares 2⅝ × 2⅝ in / 6.7 × 6.7 cm, to give sixteen pieced squares. Follow the instructions which accompany the Chickengirl quilt on page 25 to make 16 half-square triangles.

5. Press the units open, then sew into two strips of eight squares each for the sawtooth side borders.

6. Add a 2½ in / 6.4 cm wide strip to each side of the bird block. Follow the piecing diagram and assemble the oak leaf and plain strips to make the center rectangle.

7. Adjust the length of the sawtooth strips before sewing to the sides. Adjust the patchwork panel to fit the lining and wadding panels cut earlier. You may need to add more horizontal strips.

MAKING THE BAG

1. Make up two handles by pressing under ½ in / 1.3 cm on the long sides of both handle strips. Lay a strip of

wadding along each handle, tucking it under the turning. Press ½ in / 1.3 cm turning at both short ends.

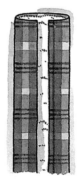

To complete the handles, fold the strips in half lengthwise and tack together thoroughly. Machine topstitch on all four sides. Reinforce the ends with a bartack.

2. To make up the tab, place the two rectangles RS together on top of the wadding and pin the paper pattern on top. Sew all around following the edge of the paper leaving an opening on one straight side for turning inside out. Cut out leaving ¼ in/0.6 cm seam allowance.

Turn to the RS, carefully pressing the edges and sew closed. Machine topstitch ¼ in/0.6 cm from the edge. Work two buttonholes in the marked positions.

3. To make up the bag, make a sandwich of one piece of wadding,

the bag back with RS up, the bag front with RS down and then the second piece of wadding. Machine sew around the sides and bottom of the bag but do not turn through yet.

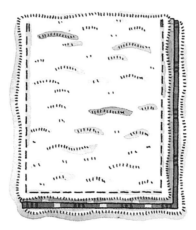

Place the two lining pieces RS together and sew around the sides and bottom. Place the lining on one side of the bag, matching the bottom corners where the two can be held together with a stitch between their seam allowances. This will hold the lining when you turn the bag RS out.

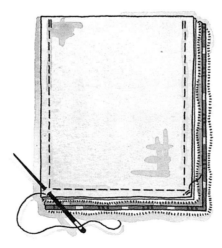

4. Turn the bag right side out and tack the top edges together. Fold over about ½ in/1.3 cm on one short

end of the binding strip and lay it along the top edge of the bag with raw edge about ½ in/1.3 cm from the top of the bag. Machine sew ¼ in/0.6 cm from the edge of the binding, and continue stitching until you overlap the start.

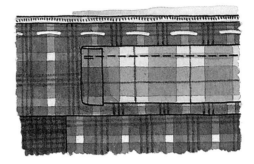

Trim if necessary, then fold the binding over to the inside. Turn under ¼ in/0.6 cm seam allowance and hem in place.

5. Position the ends of the handles about 4½ in/11.5 cm apart on each side of the bag. Tack in place, then machine stitch through all layers. Fold the tab over the top of the bag, mark the button positions and sew the buttons on securely with a short shank. If you are concerned that the tab may become lost after buttoning it onto the back of the bag, the buttonhole can be sewn closed around the button shank.

Child's Log Cabin Bag

Quick to make as a gift for a child, this bag is also easy enough to be
made by a child with a bit of help with the appliqué, if necessary. Use any motif that
will fit comfortably in a 4½ in/11.4 cm square. The addition of a buttoned
security tab will prevent belongings falling out when the bag is dropped in a hurry!

SIZE   14½ × 11 in/36.8 × 28 cm

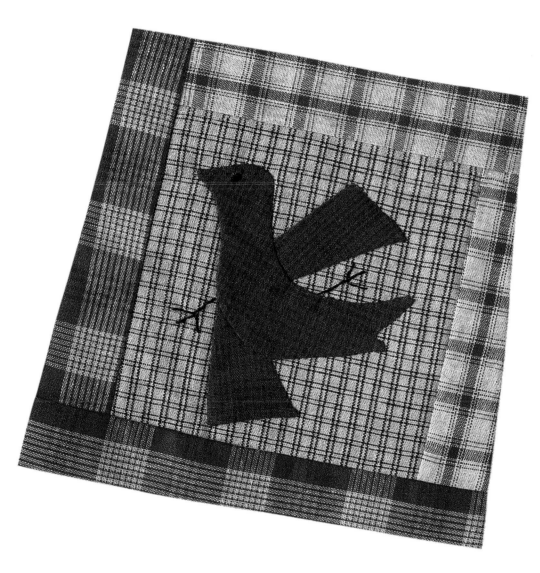

MATERIALS

Lining: two pieces each 15 × 12 in/
38 × 30.5 cm

Wadding: two pieces each 15 × 12 in/
38 × 30.5 cm, one piece 6 × 4½ in/
15.2 × 11.5 cm for tab, two strips
13½ × 1 in/34.3 × 2.5 cm for inside
handles

Plain crimson: two pieces 11½ × 3 in/
29.5 × 7.5 cm for top border

Red and black plaid: one piece 11½ ×
12 in/29.5 × 30.5 cm for the back, one
strip 23½ × 2 in/60 × 5 cm for top
binding, two pieces 13½ × 3 in/
34.3 × 7.5 cm for handles, two pieces
6 × 4½ in/15.2 × 11.5 cm for tab

Beige and black plaid: one square
5 × 5 in/12.7 × 12.7 cm

Assorted scraps for log cabin strips
and appliqué bird

Embroidery thread for eye and legs

One or two buttons

PATTERNS

Make templates for the skittish bird from the Old Homestead quilt to measure 3¾ in/9.5 cm high. Make a paper pattern for the tab.

CUTTING

1. Cut out the bag pieces as listed in Materials. Also cut some strips for the log cabin patchwork around the central block.

2. Cut out the bird motif.

SEWING

1. Appliqué the bird onto the 5 in/12.5 cm square.

2. Embroider the eye and legs.

3. Divide the fabrics for the log cabin patchwork into two groups – this can be done by color or by value. Strips from one group will be sewn to two adjacent sides of the square and strips from the second group will be sewn on the remaining two sides. Place the first strip on one side of the appliqué block, RS

together, with raw edges even and sew, taking ¼ in/0.6 cm seam.

4. Press open, then repeat with a second strip of the same fabric on the next side.

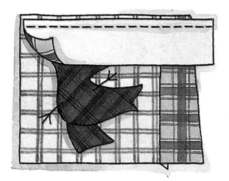

If you are working with scraps for the logs, you may need to trim them after they have been sewn in place.

Choose a fabric from the second group to add the next two strips in the same way. Notice that the strips vary in width both from one another and along their length to create a random appearance.

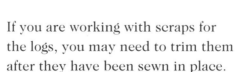

Continue adding strips until the block measures 12 × 11½ in/ 30.5 × 29.5 cm, trimming as necessary. To finish the front and back, sew a strip of crimson to the top edge of the front panel, and to the top of the red and black plaid fabric.

MAKING THE BAG

Follow the directions on page 17 for making up the bag.

Christmas Wallhanging

SIZE 12½ × 10 in/31.8 × 25.4 cm

MATERIALS

21 × 12½ in/53 × 31.8 cm backing
15 × 12½ in/38 × 31.8 cm wadding
Fat eighth yd/m red for binding, berries
8 × 7 in/20.3 × 17.8 cm plaid for bird
Scraps for appliqués, piecing, points
10 bells approx. ⅜ in/10 mm
Embroidery thread for details

METHOD

● Make templates for mistletoe and holly; bird from Homestead quilt; star and moon from Marriage quilt.

● Cut a 6 × 12½ in/15 × 31.8 cm strip from the top of backing fabric for hanging sleeve. Cut two binding strips each 14 × 1 in/35.5 × 2.5 cm and one strip 11 × 1 in/28 × 2.5 cm. From scraps cut a few small patches 2 in/5 cm wide for side borders, a few 2½ in/6.4 cm wide for top and bottom borders and a strip 6½ × 1 in/16.5 cm × 2.5 cm for the lower edge of the bird block. Cut all the appliqué motifs from scraps. Cut ten rectangles each 1½ × 1 in/3.8 × 2.5 cm for the prairie points.

● Appliqué bird to background, embroider eye and legs. Trim block to 7½ × 6½ in/19 × 16.5 cm. Add lower strip. Apply motifs except mistletoe.

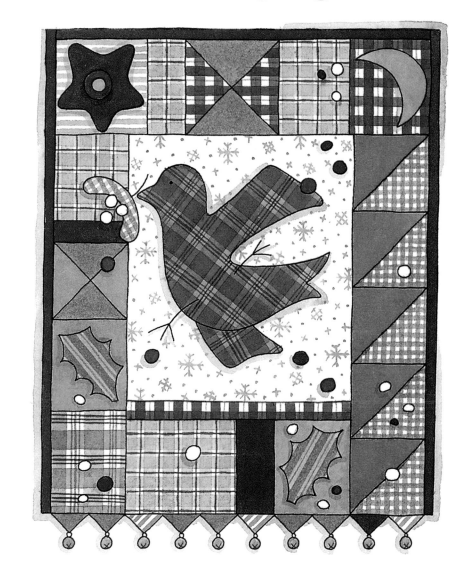

Work three units of half-square triangle blocks as in the Chickengirl quilt, marking out squares 2⅞ × 2⅞ in/7.3 × 7.3 cm. Work hourglass blocks as in the Marriage quilt, marking squares 3¾ × 3¾ in/ 9.6 × 9.6 cm. Combine these with the little appliqué blocks and other patches to make up four borders. Attach the lower border first, then the side borders and top one. Apply mistletoe, snowflakes, berries.

Prepare the prairie points as in the Shepherd quilt. Position them along lower edge of hanging, with raw edges level and points facing towards top of the hanging. Tack.

Put hanging and backing RS together. Place wadding over. Sew all layers along lower edges. Turn backing and wadding over to the back of the hanging. Quilt, then bind the remaining three sides. Sew bells to points.

Chickengirl Quilt

The lively central panel of the Chickengirl rescuing her charge from the clutches of a curious fox

is anchored by appliqué blocks of three cautious hens on their nesting boxes. The

flutter and flurry of the startled bird resonates with great wit in the choice of the Birds in the Air border

blocks. The quilt is worked in an assortment of blues and rich browns set against

a pale ground. The busy border offers a wonderful opportunity to dig deep into your scrap bag.

SIZE   85½ × 63 in / 217.2 × 160 cm

MATERIALS

● Yardage requirements for the plaid fabrics only are based on 60 in/ 150 cm wide Mission Valley fabrics.

90 × 70 in / 228.6 × 178 cm backing fabric

90 × 70 in / 228.6 × 178 cm wadding

35 × 44 in / 89 × 111.8 cm light background for center panel

1 yd / 1 m light blue plaid for border and sashing

½ yd / 0.5 m matching light blue stripe for sashing and girl's trousers

½ yd / 0.5 m light beige or tea-dyed calico for blocks, sashing and piecing

1 yd / 1 m mid blue plain for block backgrounds, sashing squares, pieced blocks and appliqué

¼ yd / 0.25 m each of navy, dark brown, tan, light yellow print, white-on-calico, old gold, mid brown,

chestnut, red & beige plaid, fine rust with black plaid, black with rust plaid, beige & black plaid, light brick red, garnet red, grey-green, light blue-grey, light yellow and one print containing some of these colors

Scraps of unbleached calico, crimson and peach

Embroidery thread for details

Sewing thread

PATTERNS

Make templates according to your chosen appliqué technique for the girl, both foxes, nesting hen, feeding hen and the chick as indicated in the template section. Note that the hat and boots in the lower left block are the same size as those on the central panel. Make your own flowers and bush using the quilt as a guide.

CUTTING

1. From the light blue plaid cut 42 strips 9½ × 3½ in/24.2 × 8.9 cm for the border and sashing.

2. From matching stripe cut two 2 in/5 cm strips across the full width of the fabric to frame the central panel and two more strips 2 × 33½ in/5 × 85.1 cm for the top and bottom. Cut strips from the light beige or tea-dyed fabric to make up the same lengths. You may have to

join strips depending on the width of your fabric to make up these inner borders. For the triangle border cut one strip 33½ × 3 in/85.1 × 7.6 cm from each of these fabrics. Cut two strips 12½ × 2 in/31.8 × 5 cm from the striped fabric only for sashing between the three nesting hens.

3. Cut the following block backgrounds:
three 12½ × 10½ in/31.8 × 26.7 cm of mid blue for nesting hens
two 9½ × 9½ in/24.2 × 24.2 cm of mid blue for feeding hen and sleeping fox
one 9½ × 9½ in/24.2 × 24.2 cm of beige & black for three chicks
one 9½ × 9½ in/24.2 × 24.2 cm of tea-dyed/beige for hat & boots
one 6½ × 6½ in/16.5 × 16.5 cm of tea-dyed/beige for two chicks
one 6½ × 6½ in/16.5 × 16.5 cm of blue-grey for chick
one 6½ × 6½ in/16.5 × 16.5 cm of grey-green for chick
one 3½ × 3½ in/8.9 × 8.9 cm of black with rust for little flower

4. For the centers of the setting squares cut ten mid blue, ten tan, four navy and four light yellow print each 2 × 2 in/5 × 5 cm squares. Cut strips 1¼ in/3.2 cm wide to total 88 in/223.5 cm of mid blue and 110 in/279.4 cm each of navy and dark brown for the setting squares.

5. Cut all the appliqué shapes following the photograph of the Chickengirl quilt on page 23 as a guide for the position of the motifs and the choice of colors.

6. The half-square triangle units for the Birds in the Air blocks are quick-pieced using a method where they are marked and stitched before being cut. Detailed instructions follow in the next section.

SEWING

1. Work the central panel appliqué, the nesting hen blocks, the corner blocks and the little blocks which will be added to the pieced blocks. Once you have completed the appliqué, check the size of the central panel and if necessary trim to measure 42½ × 33½ in/108 × 85.1 cm.

2. To prepare the triangle border first mark the RS top edge of the stripe fabric at intervals of 1½ in/3.8 cm. These marks are alternately the top point of a triangle and the cutting line between the triangles. Lay the marked strip over the matching tea-dyed/beige strip, both RS up and tack together along the unmarked edges.

Tack or pin again close to the marked edge. Fold under the left-hand end towards the first mark from a point about ¼ in/0.6 cm up from the bottom and allowing for a similar turning at the top point. Begin to appliqué this first fold and take an extra securing stitch at the point. Next, at the second mark cut into the top fabric to within about ¼ in/0.6 cm of the bottom edge.

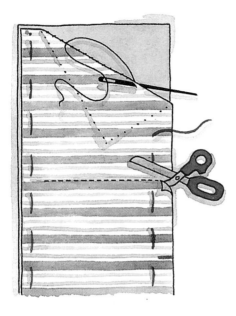

Now fold the second side of the triangle under and sew. Proceed in this manner, cutting and sewing one section at a time.

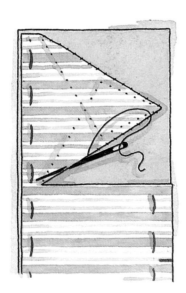

Don't make all the cuts at the start as they become difficult to control and will fray with over-handling.

The aim is to have all the top points level with one another. Press the border when finished, then sew to the bottom edge of the central panel. Sew the narrow strip of white-on-calico to the lower edge of the triangle border.

3. Work the setting squares next. Sew a 1¼ in/3.2 cm strip to two opposite sides of a center square. Press open, then sew strips to the two remaining sides. Press again.

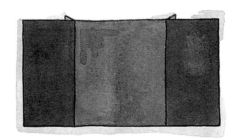

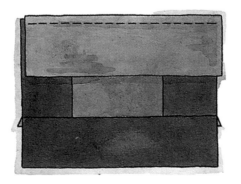

Make up setting squares in these combinations:
four light yellow centers framed with mid blue strips

four navy centers framed with mid blue strips
ten mid blue centers framed with navy strips
ten tan centers framed with dark brown strips.

4. To make the Birds in the Air blocks work quick-pieced half-square triangles. On the WS of a suitably sized piece of fabric mark out a square $3\frac{7}{8} \times 3\frac{7}{8}$ in/9.9×9.9 cm, and mark one diagonal. Place RS together with the second fabric and sew ¼ in/0.6 cm away from both sides of the diagonal. Cut the square out and cut along the marked diagonal between the stitching. Press units open. This makes two pieced units from each square drawn.

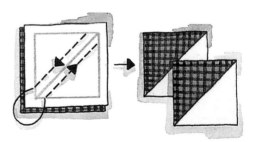

It is easiest to mark up the lighter of the two fabrics, and where you want several in the same combination the squares can be drawn as a grid as in the illustration below, putting the diagonals in opposite directions in neighboring squares.

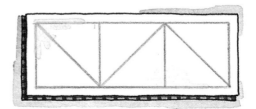

To avoid having too many of any one combination, it is best to make no more than three squares of fabric pairs, making six identical units. Notice that each of the Birds in the Air blocks needs units with a light triangle in a particular position to create the pattern.

Eighty of these light triangle units are needed. Piece these first, then have fun trying how many combinations you can make with the leftover scraps. Fifty-one units of medium and dark fabrics are needed. Arrange the half-square triangles with the smaller appliqué blocks into attractive blocks. Pin, then sew together making sure the appliqués are the right way up.

5. Following the illustration, lay out all the units of the quilt ready to sew together. Make sure to put the pieced blocks in the borders with the light patches facing the right direction. Sew the nesting hen blocks together with their sashing strips and join to the bottom of the white-on-calico strip. Sew together the pairs of the inner border and attach the two longer ones, one to each side of the center unit. Join a yellow-centered setting square to each end of the shorter inner border. Stitch these to the top and bottom edges of the center. Join together sashing strips and blocks for the two side borders and attach

to the center. Assemble the upper and lower borders of pieced blocks and sashing strips. Assemble the top and bottom rows of setting squares and sashing strips, then attach these in the correct sequence.

6. On a flat surface spread out the backing, RS down, and the wadding and prepared top, RS up. Pin, then tack the layers together. Quilt in-the-ditch around the appliqués, the light triangles of the patchwork blocks, the setting square centers and the borders.

7. Fold-finish the edges as directed in the General Techniques chapter.

Kitchen Chicks Apron

Cheer up your cooking sessions with a brood of chicks appliquéd on this easy-to-make apron.

With matching oven mitts (see page 30) together they make a charming gift for a kitchen

tea. The simple appliqué shapes are ideal for the quick and easy starch preparation method. Using blanket

stitch to secure the chicks, this project can be successfully completed in a day.

SIZE   27 in long × 21 in across/68.5 × 53 cm

MATERIALS

¾ yd/0.75 m plaid for apron, pocket, neckband and ties

¼ yd/0.25 m contrast plain fabric for binding

Scraps of contrast plain fabric for appliqué shapes

Embroidery threads

PATTERNS

Make a template for the chick motif from the Chickengirl quilt. The chick body needs to be 3 in/7.5 cm tall, not counting the legs. Make a full-size paper pattern of the apron and pocket pieces from the patterns provided on pages 122 and 123. The correct pocket position has been marked on the pattern.

CUTTING

1. Fold the fabric lengthwise 12 in/ 30.5 cm from one edge. Place the apron pattern on the fold and cut.

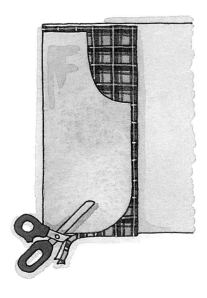

From the remaining fabric cut one pocket and three strips 27 × 3 in/ 68.6 × 7.5 cm.

2. Using the contrast fabric make continuous bias binding following the instructions in the General Techniques chapter, cutting strips 1 in/2.5 cm wide.

3. From the contrasting scraps, cut the appliqué motifs appropriate for your chosen technique.

SEWING

1. Appliqué the chicks on the pocket and the apron bib. Embroider the flower centers and the chicks' legs, eyes and beaks. They will look better if the embroidered features are different.

2. Machine the binding to the top straight edge of the pocket, then turn over to the WS and hem. Bind the remaining curved edge, tidying the ends carefully. Using the illustration as a guide, place the pocket on the apron, pin or tack, then machine in position close to the binding on the curved edge. Reinforce the start and finish with a bartack and work another one at the center of the pocket top edge.

3. On each of the long strips, press under ½ in/1.3 cm along both long sides. On two of them also press under a turning on one short end: these will become the waist ties. Now press the strips in half lengthways. Topstitch through the layers close to the pressed edges.

4. Put the apron RS down and on each side, pin or tack the raw end of one tie about ¼ in/0.6 cm down from the side corner of the apron, having the raw end level with the side of the apron. Sew securely in place within the seam allowance before binding the curved side and lower edge of the apron, enclosing the ends of the ties as you do so.

5. Bind the curved sides of the bib. From the remaining prepared long strip cut about 24 in/61 cm for the neckband (or measure the person and cut length accordingly). Lay the apron RS down and position the ends of the neckband in a similar way to the ties, close to the side binding. Straighten the neckband before anchoring the ends in the seam allowance. Bind the top edge to complete.

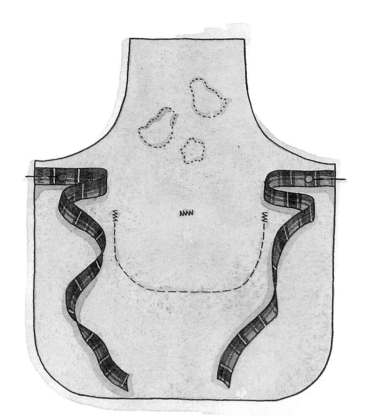

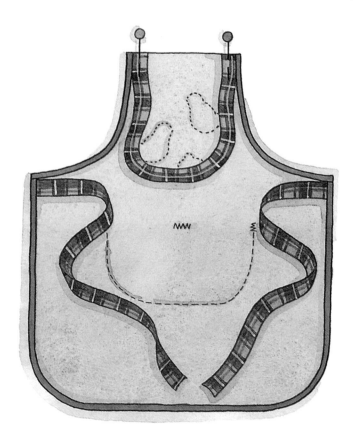

Kitchen Chicks Oven Mitts

Designed to team up with the apron, the oven mitt is a simple project that can be decorated freely with chicks and motifs from other projects in the book. The mitt can be padded with just wadding for the back and lower palm section; however, if you can find a thicker padding, such as a piece of old blanket, for the upper palm, this will provide better heat protection.

SIZE   11½ × 6½ in / 29 × 16.5 cm

MATERIALS

For two mitts:
¼ yd / 0.25 m plaid fabric
15 × 10 in / 38 × 25.4 cm contrast for mitt palms
¼ yd / 0.25 m contrast plain for binding

½ yd / 0.5 m padding for the mitts
¼ yd / 0.25 m lining
Scraps in contrasting plains for appliqué shapes
Embroidery threads

PATTERNS

Make a template for the chick motif from the Chickengirl single quilt. The chick body needs to be 3 in / 7.5 cm tall, not including the legs. Make a paper pattern for pieces A, B and C. Extra wide ½ in / 1.3 cm seam allowances are included in the mitt pattern to cope with the extra thickness during making.

CUTTING

1. For each mitt, cut one each of pieces A and C in the main plaid fabric and one of piece B in the contrast for mitt upper palm. Cut one of each piece A, B and C in lining and wadding, with an extra layer for the upper palm if desired.

2. Following the directions in the General Techniques chapter, turn the contrast plain fabric into continuous bias binding, cutting the strips 1¼ in / 3.2 cm wide.

3. Cut the chick and flower motifs from the contrasting plain scraps.

SEWING

1. Appliqué the motifs on the back (piece A) of the oven mitt.

2. Assemble the layers for pieces A, B and C, with the lining RS down and the wadding and outer fabric RS up. Pin and tack the layers together then channel quilt following the lines of the plaid as a guide. The motifs on the back can be outline quilted by hand or by machine, if you wish.

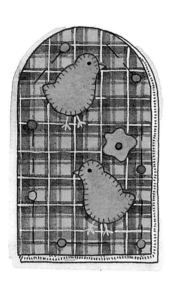

3. After quilting, machine around each piece ⅜ in/1 cm from the raw edge, except on the lower straight edges of pieces A and C.

4. Bind the straight edges, taking just a ¼ in/0.6 cm seam.

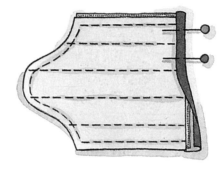

5. Place the two palm sections together. With RS facing and notches matching, sew the curved, notched edge using a ½ in/1.3 cm seam allowance. Clip the curve and turn RS out.

6. Lay the back and palm, linings together. Check that the two bound lower edges are even, and sew through all layers, ⅜ in/1 cm from the raw edges but leaving the bound edges open. Trim away ¼ in/0.6 cm around the raw edge, and snip extra wadding from between the layers to reduce the bulk.

7. Bind the raw edges, leaving an extra tail of binding, about 6 in/15.2 cm long, on one side. Attach the binding to the mitt back with a ¼ in/0.6 cm seam, then fold it over to the palm and hem in place. Fold and sew the binding tail to the mitt to make a hanging loop.

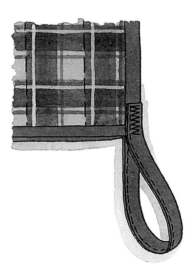

Dancing Couples Wallhanging

By the skillful organization of many different dark and light fabrics this wallhanging achieves a wonderful sense of depth and a very painterly quality. This piece was worked using needle-turned appliqué except for the distant figures which were applied with fusible web. If you decide to work more of the project using bonded appliqué, you will need to adjust your material requirements. This wallhanging is a thoroughly enjoyable project to make, and you should have lots of fun building the distant hills, the road and the foreground hill from a wide selection of directional fabrics such as plaids and stripes.

SIZE 36 × 26 in / 91.5 × 66 cm

MATERIALS

1 yd / 1 m backing

40 × 30 in / 101.5 × 76.2 cm wadding

¼ yd / 0.25 m each dark print/plain for binding and plain plum for inner border

½ yd / 0.5 m dark plum plaid for shacks, middle border and remainder for piecing hills

½ yd / 0.5 m dark blue plaid for sky

¼ yd / 0.25 m plain black for silhouettes, cats and boots

Assorted scraps of dark, medium and light plaids and stripes for the pieced landscape

Assorted fabrics for the appliqués including warm beige, terracotta, "clothing" prints and plaids, plain old gold, peach, geranium and rose pinks, tan and yellow

Embroidery threads for details

A scrap of fusible web for the distant figures

PATTERNS

A full-size pattern of the whole design is essential to work this project successfully. Make templates for the appliqué motifs: the couple-and-shack group, the distant silhouettes, the star and moon, the dog and cockerel as appropriate for the appliqué method to be used. You may use templates for the landscape or not depending on the technique you choose.

CUTTING

1. From binding fabric cut four strips 2 in/5 cm wide across the fabric. Cut four plain plum strips 1 in/2.5 cm wide for inner border.

From the dark plum plaid cut four strips each 1¼ in/3.2 cm wide across the fabric for the middle border. Cut four corner squares each 1¼ × 1¼ in/3.2 × 3.2 cm from the geranium pink scraps.

2. Following the manufacturer's instructions, trace the distant couple in reverse on the paper side of the fusible web. Bond to the WS of the black fabric and cut out.

3. From the dark plum plaid cut two shacks, one with the template as is, and one reversed.

4. Cut the remaining appliqué pieces, remembering to cut one set in reverse for the main group consisting of shack, cat, man and

woman. Cut the tree in branches as marked to avoid sewing tight inside corners. For the rooftops, cut as a straight line. When sewing, snip at regular intervals and fold in to create the serrated edge as described for the triangle border in the Chickengirl quilt.

5. Build up the background landscape by following the instructions in the Apple Picker quilt, cutting each piece as you go. Use a paper or muslin foundation to stabilize the work during construction. If using a paper foundation work each area on a separate paper. Alternatively, you can draw out each piece following our design, make templates, then cut and piece in the conventional way.

SEWING

1. Work the background landscape following the directions in the Apple Picker quilt, working from the top down. Pin the sky fabric over your foundation paper. Apply the smaller shapes on top, then place the final two shapes in position.

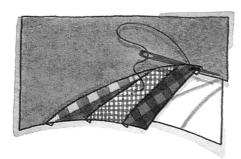

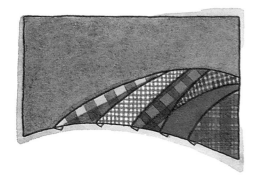

If you prefer working on smaller units, you can apply the moon, star, dog and silhouettes when the sky and furthest hill have been assembled, before adding the rest of the landscape.

When complete, press and check the size. Use rows of tacking stitches to mark the top and bottom position of the figures. Do not trim until they have been sewn.

2. Add the appliquéd groups, starting with the shack, roof and gutter. Follow with the cat, cowboy and lastly the woman. Cut away areas behind these groups as you go to ensure a smooth appearance.

Embroider all the details.

3. Press and check the size of the central panel, trimming as necessary to measure 32 × 22½ in/ 81.3 × 57.3 cm. Sew the plum strips to opposite sides of the central panel. Press, then sew on remaining borders. Press again.

4. Add strips of dark plum plaid to the sides of the quilt. Press outer border. Trim remaining dark plum plaid borders to measure 23½ in/ 59.7 cm. Add a geranium pink corner square to each end of the top and bottom borders. Now sew these to the quilt.

5. Press the top carefully. Trim away any loose threads.

6. For the backing cut a 40 × 30 in/ 101.5 × 76.2 cm rectangle. Spread the backing RS down, center the wadding and top RS up on a flat surface. Pin or tack the layers together. To emphasize elements in the picture, quilt in-the-ditch around selected motifs. Quilt one of the border seams.

7. Attach the binding strips. Fold the binding to the back of the wallhanging and hem in place.

8. From the remaining backing fabric, cut, sew and attach a hanging sleeve as described in the General Techniques chapter.

Country Cushions

Four cheerful country cushions to make a welcome addition to any sofa or kitchen chairs.

The large, simple motifs make them ideal projects for beginners, and

any newcomer to appliqué would find them quite manageable and very rewarding.

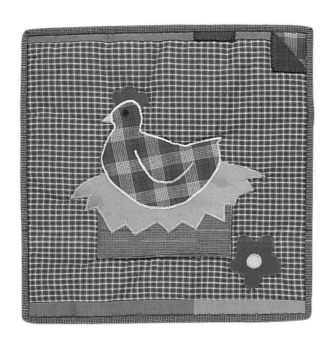
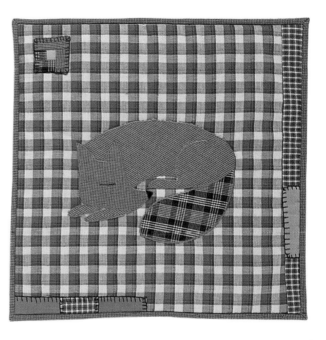

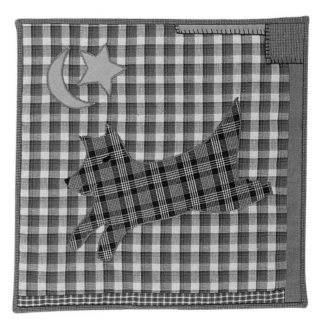

Dancing Dog Cushion

This cushion features the dancing dog from of the Dancing Couples wallhanging. I have simply

placed it on a plaid background, and with the addition of a few assorted

patches randomly placed around the edges, the cushion captures a truly homespun look.

Size   15 × 15 in / 38 × 38 cm

MATERIALS

½ yd / 0.5 m plaid for the cushion front and back

16 × 16 in / 40.7 × 40.7 cm calico or similar to line the front

16 × 16 in / 40.7 × 40.7 cm wadding

¼ yd / 0.25 m for binding

¼ yd / 0.25 m fusible web

12 × 8 in / 30.5 × 20.3 cm contrast plaid for the dog

Gold scraps for the moon and star

Assorted small scraps for the edge patches

Embroidery thread for the blanket stitch on the patches

Machine embroidery thread for the bonded appliqué

PATTERNS

From the Dancing Couples design, make templates for the moon, stars and dog. The crescent should measure 3¼ in / 8.3 cm straight across from tip to tip. The dog should measure 11 in / 28 cm from front paws to back.

CUTTING

1. For the cushion front cut a square 15½ × 15½ in / 39.5 × 39.5 cm. From the same green plaid fabric cut two pieces 10½ × 15½ in / 26.7 × 39.5 cm for the overlapped cushion back.

2. For the binding, cut straight-grain strips 2 in / 5 cm wide to total about 64 in / 162 cm length, joining the strips as necessary.

3. Following the instructions in the General Techniques chapter for bonded appliqué, trace the dog motif, the moon and star onto the paper side of the fusible web, reversing the designs to do so.

4. Cut out and bond to the WS of your chosen fabrics.

5. Allow to cool completely before cutting out carefully along the pencil line.

SEWING

1. Remove the paper from the bonded motifs, position them with the bonded side down on the RS of the cushion front and fuse into place using a damp cloth and hot iron.

2. Allow to cool fully before working satin stitch around the motifs, using a contrasting color thread. Blanket stitch if you prefer. When sewing sharp points, use the variable width control on the machine if you have one to obtain the most pleasing effect.

3. Add a few extra patches of various fabrics around the edges of the front of the cushion. Do this by machine, sewing a strip on with RS together, then flipping it over and pressing into place.

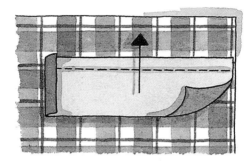

Alternatively, sew by hand, pressing raw edges under, then sewing into place with blanket stitch.

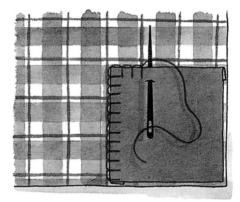

No patterns or sizes are given so you can decide according to your available scraps. When complete, press carefully.

4. Place the calico lining on a flat surface, center the wadding over it and put the cushion front, RS up, on top. Pin or tack the layers together for quilting.

5. Outline quilt the motifs. Add more quilting to the background if

you wish. An easy method is to follow some of the lines of the plaid. After quilting, tack around the four sides of the panel close to the edge.

6. Trim away the excess wadding and lining.

7. Press under ½ in/1.3 cm along one long side of each piece of cushion backs and machine in place. Lay the prepared cushion front on a flat surface RS down, and position the backs RS up, over the front so that the raw edges are even with the edges of the front and the hemmed edges overlap across the middle. Sew all layers together on all four sides just within the ¼ in/0.6 cm seam allowance.

8. Fold the binding strip in half lengthwise to make a double binding for finishing the edge of the cushion, as directed in the General Techniques chapter.

Cockerel Cushion

Worked in a pair of bold, dark plaids, our cockerel, proudly strutting under the bright yellow
moon and star, makes a great partner for the nesting hen.

SIZE   15 × 15 in / 38 × 38 cm

MATERIALS

½ yd / 0.5 m plaid for the cushion front
and back.

16 × 16 in / 40.7 × 40.7 cm calico or
similar to line the front

16 × 16 in / 40.7 × 40.7 cm wadding

¼ yd / 0.25 m for binding

½ yd / 0.5 m fusible web

Assorted scraps for the cockerel's
body, wings, comb, wattle and beak,
the moon, star and the edge patches

Embroidery thread for the blanket
stitch on the patches

Machine embroidery thread for the
bonded appliqué

PATTERNS

Make templates for the moon, star
and cockerel from the Dancing
Couples wallhanging. The crescent
should measure 3¼ in / 8.3 cm
straight across from tip to tip. The
cockerel should measure about
9¼ in / 23.5 cm from chest to tail.

CUTTING

1. For the cushion front cut a
square 15½ × 15½ in / 39.5 ×
39.5 cm. From the same fabric, cut
two pieces 10½ × 15½ in / 26.7 ×
39.5 cm for the overlapped sections
of the cushion back.

2. For the binding, cut straight-
grain strips 2 in / 5 cm wide to total
about 64 in / 162 cm length, joining
the strips as necessary.

3. Following the instructions in the
General Techniques chapter (page
108) for bonded appliqué, trace the
cockerel, moon and star onto the
paper side of the fusible web,
reversing the designs to do so. Cut
out and iron to the WS of your
chosen fabrics.

4. Allow to cool completely before
cutting out carefully along the
pencil lines.

SEWING

Follow the instructions on page 39
to make up the cushion.

Nesting Hen Cushion

The nesting hen block features as a main appliqué motif on the Chickengirl quilt. I have worked the cushion in a variety of plaids of varying scale with a sprinkling of strong colors for definition.

SIZE   15 × 15 in / 38 × 38 cm

MATERIALS

½ yd / 0.5 m plaid for the cushion front and back

16 × 16 in / 40.7 × 40.7 cm calico or similar to line the front

16 × 16 in / 40.7 × 40.7 cm wadding

¼ yd / 0.25 m for binding

½ yd / 0.5 m fusible web

Assorted scraps for the hen, her beak and comb, the straw, the nestbox, the flower and the edge patches

Embroidery thread for blanket stitch on the patches

Machine embroidery thread for bonded appliqué

PATTERNS

The motif on the cushion illustrated measures 10½ in / 26.5 cm at the widest point across the straw. Check the size of the nesting hen given for the Chickengirl quilt and enlarge as necessary or to suit your preference.

CUTTING

1. For the cushion front cut a square 15½ × 15½ in / 39.5 × 39.5 cm. From the same fabric cut two pieces 10½ × 15½ in / 26.7 × 39.5 cm for the overlapped sections of the cushion back.

2. For the binding cut straight-grain strips 2 in / 5 cm wide to total about 64 in / 162 cm length, joining as necessary.

3. Following the instructions in the General Techniques chapter for bonded appliqué, trace all parts of the hen motif and a flower shape onto the paper side of the fusible web, reversing the designs to do so. Cut out and bond to the WS of your chosen fabrics.

4. Allow to cool completely before cutting out carefully.

SEWING

Follow the instructions on page 39 for making up the cushion.

41

Sleeping Fox Cushion

Our fox looks so peaceful sleeping on this cushion. He is one of the corner block designs on the Chickengirl quilt. Make him in two different fabrics for best effect.

SIZE   15 × 15 in / 38 × 38 cm

MATERIALS

½ yd / 0.5 m plaid for the cushion front and back

16 × 16 in / 40.7 × 40.7 cm calico or similar to line the front

16 × 16 in / 40.7 × 40.7 cm wadding

¼ yd / 0.25 m for binding

¼ yd / 0.25 m fusible web

10 × 6 in / 25.4 × 15.2 cm contrast plaid for the fox's body

6 × 5 in / 15.2 × 12.7 cm second contrast for the tail

Assorted small scraps for the edge patches

Embroidery thread for the blanket stitch on the patches

Machine embroidery thread for the bonded appliqué

PATTERNS

Make a template for the sleeping fox as given for the Chickengirl quilt. It should measure 9 in / 22.9 cm across.

CUTTING

1. For the cushion front cut a square 15½ × 15½ in / 39.5 × 39.5 cm. From the same plaid fabric

cut two pieces 10½ × 15½ in / 26.7 × 39.5 cm for the overlapped sections of the cushion back.

2. For the binding, cut straight-grain strips 2 in / 5 cm wide to total about 64 in / 162.6 cm length, joining the strips as necessary.

3. Following the instructions in the General Techniques chapter for bonded appliqué, trace the fox body

and the tail, as two separate shapes, onto the paper side of the fusible web, reversing the designs to do so. Cut out and bond to the WS of your chosen fabrics.

4. Allow to cool completely before cutting out carefully along the pencil lines.

SEWING

Follow the instructions for making up the cushion on page 39.

Sampler Wallhanging

SIZE 22 × 27 in / 55.9 × 68.6 cm

MATERIALS

¾ yd / 0.75 m backing
26 × 30 in / 66 × 76 cm wadding
¼ yd / 0.25 m for binding
¼ yd / 0.25 m for setting strips
Assorted scraps for appliqués, piecing and border
Embroidery threads for details

METHOD

● Make templates for the corner appliqué motifs from the Goosegirl wallhanging and for the dancing dog and cockerel from the Dancing Couples wallhanging.

● From scraps cut six backgrounds for the appliqué blocks, each 5½ × 5½ in / 14 × 14 cm. Cut the appliqué motifs. Cut four setting strips 23 × 1 in / 58.5 × 2.5 cm. For the binding cut strips 2 in / 5 cm wide to a total of 102 in / 260 cm.

● Work the six appliqué blocks and embroider the details.

For the pieced blocks, work as directed for the corner four-patches (step 5) in the Marriage quilt but marking out three squares 6¼ × 6¼ in / 16 × 16 cm. Assemble these blocks, and sew a setting strip to each long side, trimming as necessary. Make two side borders each 20½ × 3¼ in / 52.2 × 8.3 cm following the instructions for the Apple Picker border (step 3) and attach to the sides of the center. Add a setting strip to top and lower edges, then make and attach borders to top and bottom to complete the quilt top.

Press the top, then spread backing RS down on a flat surface. Center the wadding, then the top over the backing. Tack, then outline quilt. Bind, attaching the strip ½ in / 1.2 cm from the raw edge and folding over to finish ½ in / 1.2 cm wide.

Apple Picker Cot Quilt

Startled by the unexpected arrival of a bluebird on her head, the young girl drops her basket of just-picked apples and all her hard work rolls away. This is a charming picture quilt with an endearing and readily accessible story which would delight both child and adult. The gentle rolling hills of the background have been machine pieced in a fairly random manner. Once you have grasped the technique of sewing these smooth long curves you can choose to create your own landscape background. The side borders are pieced from leftovers from the quilt top giving them a lovely scrap appearance that echoes the movement of the background landscape.

Size 42 × 42 in/106.7 × 106.7 cm

MATERIALS

45 × 45 in/114.3 × 114.3 cm calico for backing

45 × 45 in/114.3 × 114.3 cm lightweight wadding

½ yd/0.5 m brown plaid for binding, tree trunks and branches

½ yd/0.5 m green plaid for background piecing and leaves

½ yd/0.5 m medium dark plaid for background

¼ yd/0.25 m of further background fabrics, including one to suit the sky

¼ yd/0.25 m each of wine plaid for baskets, terracotta stripe for girls' dresses plus apples and geranium pink for apples

Two strips of white-on-calico each 42 × 1¼ in/106.7 × 3.2 cm

Scraps of dark plaid for dogs, two blues for birds, yellow for hair, warm beige for face and hands, brown for feet, and additional beiges, greens for side borders

Embroidery threads for details

PATTERNS

Make templates for the girls, tree, dog, birds and basket. For the handles use bias strips so templates are not required. The flying birds can be sewn as a single piece, or have the wing cut separately to save the less experienced stitcher from working an inside square corner. Use the same wing shape sewn over the body for the birds in the trees. The leaves are freely cut diamond shapes. An example of an apple is given but cut some variations yourself.

For the main background sketch an approximate full-size layout for the sky and land based on the illustration, keeping the curves gentle. This will be used as a foundation for sewing over so choose thin paper or muslin according to your preference.

CUTTING

1. Fabrics for the main background and side borders will be cut at the time of sewing. After completing the landscape, cut about 28 diamond leaves from the leftovers.

2. From brown plaid cut four strips 2½ × 43 in/6.4 × 109 cm and set aside for binding. From remainder cut two tree trunks (one in reverse) and three branches per tree.

3. From the terracotta cut the two-part dress for both girls. Cut two faces and three hands from the warm beige tone, two shapes of

yellow fabric for the hair and four brown triangles for the feet.

4. Cut two dogs from dark plaid, seven birds in main blue fabric and four lighter wings.

5. From basket fabric cut four baskets and four bias strips each 9 × 1 in/23 × 2.5 cm. Cut 25 apples from the geranium pink and terracotta scraps.

SEWING

1. Work the background from the top down, with each piece having spare fabric overlapping the intended edges of the quilt to be trimmed away later. Place the sky fabric over the top right of the sketch, pinning or tacking to the foundation paper or fabric, then trim leaving some seam allowance on the next edge to be covered.

2. Position fabric no. 2 and, allowing some extra for turning in, cut approximately to shape. Next, turn in the top edge to the intended curve and pin or tack in place.

3. Sew either by hand, or using the blindhem stitch on the machine, in a matching thread, close to the folded edge. If machine sewing, you may wish to use clear nylon monofilament to conceal stitching.

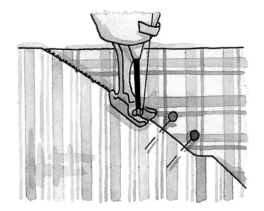

4. Press, then repeat the process for each area of the landscape. Don't expect to keep all the fabrics true to the grain of the plaid – in any case, the background will be more interesting if there are changes of angle. Be adventurous with your fabrics.

5. When the landscape is complete, add a strip of white-on-calico to each vertical side of the quilt.

6. Remove the foundation.

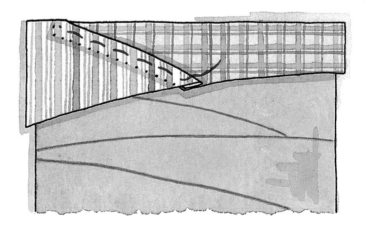

7. Work the appliqué over the background. Use a combination of appliqué techniques. Blindhem stitch small parts such as the feet and hands and use the needle-turning-under technique with a running stitch for other parts of the design.

8. To make the baskets, first sew the four groups of apples in place.

9. Work the handles by folding the bias strip in half, RS out, and pinning in place with the raw edges towards the inside curve. Sew, using a small running stitch, along the middle of the bias, which will be the outer edge of the handle, then roll the folded edge over and hem down to cover the raw edges, which may be trimmed as needed.

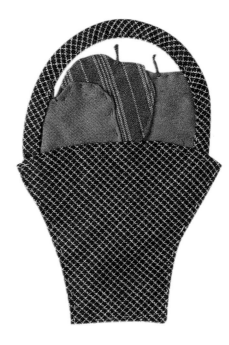

10. Position the basket over the raw edges of the handle and pin in place. Secure all round with a neat running stitch.

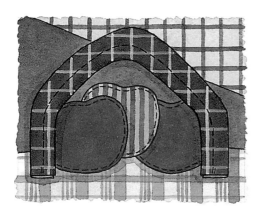

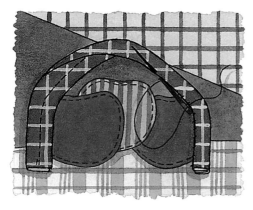

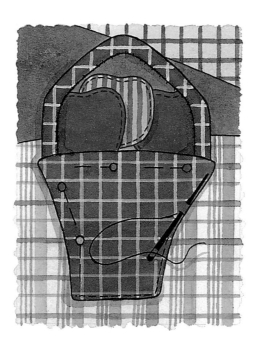

11. Study the photograph of the quilt carefully and embroider the features and apple stalks. Use a variety of stitches for added interest.

12. Work two randomly pieced side borders approximately 42 × 6 in/ 106.7 × 15.2 cm, using irregular scraps. Trim borders to measure 40¼ × 5 in/102.3 × 12.7 cm.

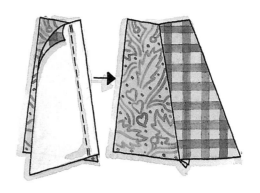

If you prefer, use a foundation to piece the random border.

13. Attach the borders. To avoid wavy bias edges, insert a line of running stitches within the seam allowance, adjusted to the correct tension to support the edges.

14. Press the quilt top carefully and trim away any loose threads.

15. On a flat surface, spread out the backing, RS down, then put the wadding and the quilt on top. Pin and tack the layers together.

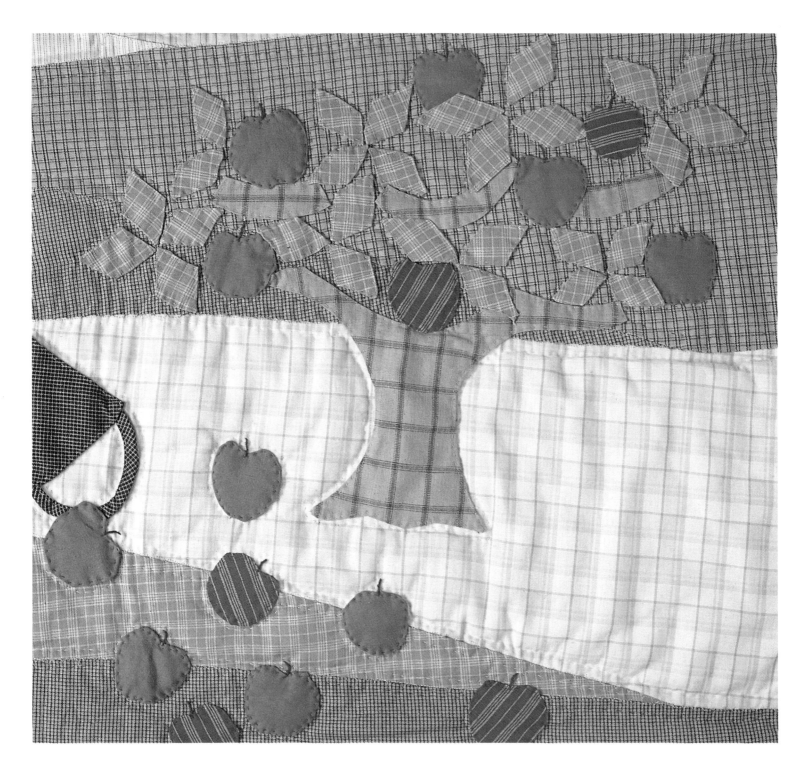

16. For added definition, outline quilt the appliqué motifs and echo quilt the main seams of the background on both sides. Echo quilt the border seams on one side only.

17. Trim the backing and wadding to extend ¾ in / 1.8 cm beyond the raw edge of the quilt top. Pin the prepared binding strips to the front of the quilt with the raw edges even.

Machine sew the binding using ¼ in / 0.6 cm seam. Fold the binding to the back of the quilt, and turn in ¼ in / 0.6 cm and hem to the machine stitching on the back.

Hit'n'Miss Picnic Rug

Perfect for picnics, this versatile "hit'n'miss" patchwork rug features appliquéd corner blocks of

baskets from the Apple Picker quilt. It makes a useful travel cushion, too, when

folded up tidily into the backing pocket. Easily pieced, this is a perfect project for beginners.

SIZE 58 × 58 in / 147 × 147 cm

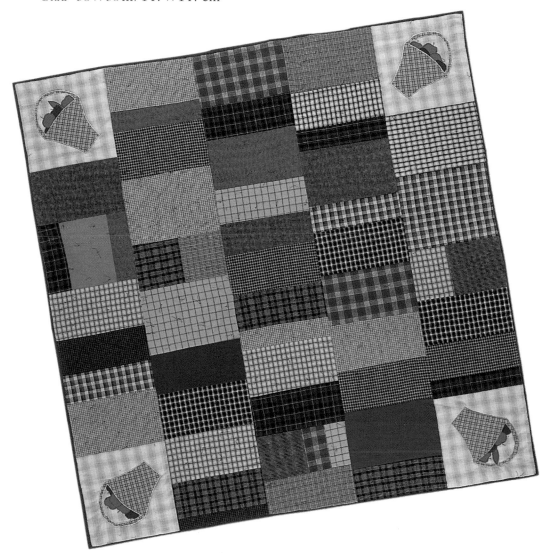

MATERIALS

2 yd × 60 in / 1.9 m × 152.4 cm wide dark backing fabric

½ yd × 60 in / 0.5 m × 152.4 cm wide light fabric for basket block background

¾ yd × 60 in / 0.7 m × 152.4 cm wide contrast dark fabric for the pocket

2 yd × 60 in / 1.9 m × 152.4 cm wide wadding

2 yd / 2 m of assorted scraps for hit'n'miss patchwork and baskets

Scraps of reds and greens for the apples in the baskets

¾ yd / 0.7m fusible web

Machine embroidery thread for appliqué

PATTERNS

Make a template for the basket and apple from the Apple Picker quilt. It should measure 9 in / 23 cm tall. Use either a photocopier or a grid to make the necessary enlargements.

CUTTING

1. From the backing fabric cut a square 60 × 60 in / 152.4 × 152.4 cm. Set aside for backing the quilt and add the remainder to the pieces for the hit'n'miss patchwork.

2. From the light block background fabric cut 5 squares each 12 × 12 in / 30.5 × 30.5 cm. Put the remainder towards the patchwork.

3. From the contrast pocket fabric cut a pocket lining 21½ × 21½ in/ 54.6 × 54.6 cm square. Cut two framing strips for the pocket each 12 × 5¼ in/30.5 × 13.3 cm and two strips each 21½ × 5¼ in/54.6 × 13.3 cm.

4. For the hit'n'miss patchwork which is made of pieced strips 12 in/30.5 cm wide, pieces need to be 12 in/30.5 cm in one direction. Cut a few rectangles of varying widths and cut more as you sew. Smaller pieces may be included by first sewing them together then trimming to 12 in/30.5 cm.

5. For the appliqué blocks follow the instructions in the General Techniques chapter for bonded appliqué. Trace the baskets and apples, plus a few leaves if you like, onto the paper side of the fusible web. Cut these out neatly then bond to the reverse of the selected fabrics and carefully cut out.

SEWING

1. Remove the paper backing from the prepared appliqué pieces and arrange them on the 12 in/30.5 cm blocks. Note that the four corner blocks have the baskets "on point" while the fifth one for the pocket has the basket set straight. Make your own arrangement of apples in and around the baskets. When happy with your designs, bond thoroughly using a damp cloth and a hot iron. Allow to cool before finishing the edges of the shapes

with machine satin stitch, or by hand using blanket stitch. Add stalks if you wish.

2. To complete the pocket front, add the short framing strips of contrast fabric to two opposite sides of the pocket block. Press, then add the remaining long strips to the other two sides and press again. Place the pocket lining, RS together, over the pocket front and sew all round leaving an opening for turning through to the right side. Press the edges out fully then machine sew closed.

3. To attach the pocket to the backing, center the pocket, basket face down, on one side of the quilt backing, with the top edge of the pocket front 1 in/2.5 cm from the edge of the backing. Topstitch around three sides of the pocket from A to B to C to D but not between A and D.

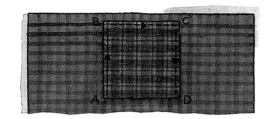

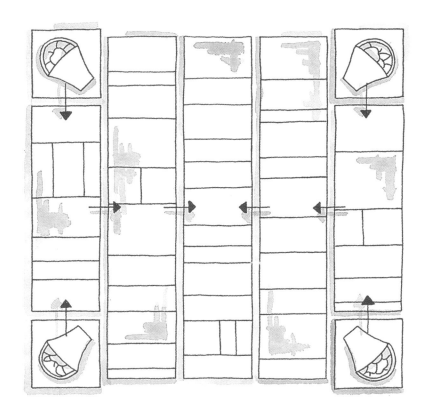

4. Using fabric scraps of varying lengths, but all 12 in/30.5 cm wide, make up three strips of hit'n'miss patchwork each 12 × 58 in/30.5 × 147.2 cm. Also make up two more strips each 12 × 34½ in/30.5 × 87.6 cm. Sew a basket corner block to each end of the two shorter strips, taking care to have the baskets angled correctly at the corners. Join all five strips together in the correct order as shown, and press.

5. Press in ½ in / 1.3 cm turning along all four sides of the backing. Lay the prepared backing, RS down, on a flat surface. Center the wadding and top over it and tack thoroughly through all layers.

6. Using either matching or contrasting embroidery thread tie the layers together at regular intervals with a square knot.

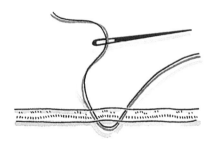

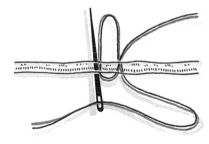

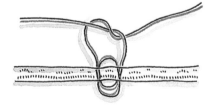

To avoid tying through the pocket by mistake, slip a piece of cardboard inside.

7. To self-bind the edges, bring the ½ in / 1.3 cm turning on the backing fabric over the raw edges of the top and sew in place. Add a few ties at intervals around the edge.

8. To store the rug inside its pocket, fold lengthwise into three with the pocket on the outside. Use the pocket as a folding guide.

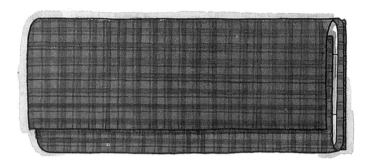

Insert your hands to find the bottom two corners and turn the pocket inside out. Fold the remaining rug into the pocket, tucking the corners in neatly. The rug should now look like a cushion.

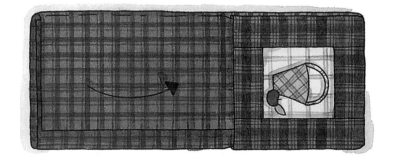

Picnic Placemats

Whether you like to entertain at home or picnic in style, these wrap-up mats are a
lovely way to present individual settings of napkin and cutlery. If you follow our example and
use a different color to bind each one, or add a different motif, not only
will they brighten up the occasion but each person will be able to identify their own.

SIZE   12½ × 10½ in/31.8 × 26.7 cm

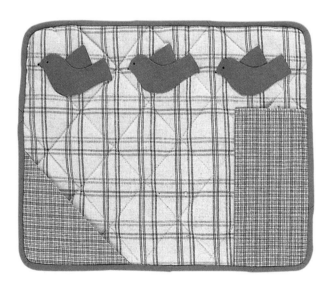
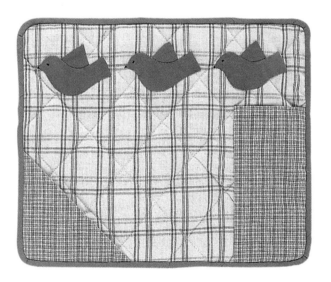
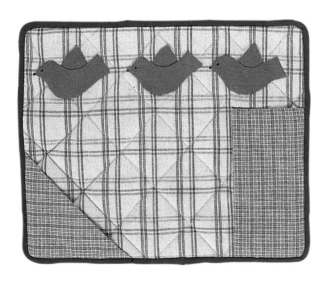
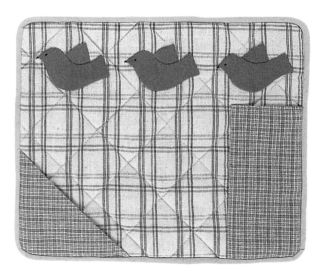

MATERIALS

Each mat requires:
12½ × 10½ in / 31.8 × 26.7 cm rectangle of background, wadding and backing
13 × 7 in / 33 × 17.7 cm matching plaid for pockets
11 × 11 in / 28 × 28 cm contrasting plain colour for binding
Scraps of plain color accent from the background for the appliqué
Embroidery thread for features

PATTERNS

Make a template of the little bluebird from the Apple Picker quilt. It should measure 3 in / 7.5 cm from beak to tail. To vary the mats, choose motifs from other projects.

CUTTING

1. The rectangles listed above are the actual sizes needed for the background, wadding and backing.

2. From the pocket fabric cut a rectangle 7 × 6½ in / 17.7 × 16.5 cm for the cutlery pocket and a square 5 × 5 in / 12.7 × 12.7 cm for the napkin pocket.

3. Turn the 11 in / 28 cm square into continuous bias binding using the method in the General Techniques chapter, cutting the bias strips 1 in / 2.5 cm wide.

4. Using the template trace the appliqué shapes and cut out three motifs per mat.

SEWING

1. Appliqué the motifs on the RS of the background fabric. Embroider the eyes and beaks.

2. Put the layers of the mat together, backing RS down, then wadding and finally the top, RS up. Tack and quilt.

3. To prepare the napkin pocket, fold the 5 in / 12.7 cm square lightly on the diagonal, RS out. Unfold, then machine staystitch about ¼ in / 0.6 cm to one side of the crease.

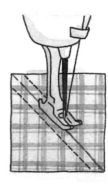

Refold and place on the lower left corner of the background, having the stitched side facing the background and the two raw edges even. Tack in place.

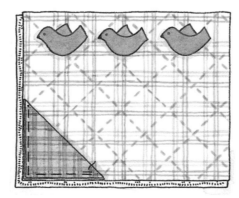

4. If you choose to add the cutlery pocket, press under, then stitch a narrow hem on one long side of the 7 × 6½ in / 17.7 × 16.5 cm prepared rectangle.

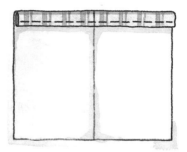

Fold in half and fingerpress a crease at right angles to the hem. Place RS down on the lower right corner of the quilted mat with the two raw edges level, and sew along the marked crease.

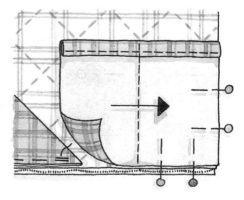

Fold the loose end over towards the corner of the mat.

Sew the two layers of the pocket together at the top. Place the pocket in position, raw edges even, and tack to the edge of the mat.

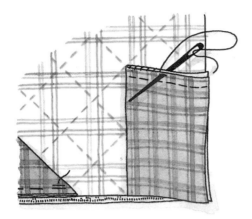

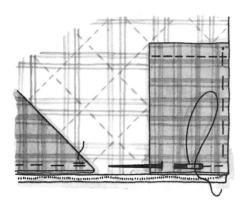

5. Cut a bias strip 29 in/74 cm for the ties. Press in ¼ in/0.6 cm on both long sides, then press in half and machine stitch.

Fold the bias in two, unevenly (for easier tying). Stitch with the fold to the raw edge of the mat on the back at the napkin pocket end 6¼ in/16 cm up from the bottom.

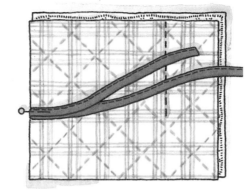

6. Trace around a spool of thread to mark the rounded corners of the mat. Machine the remaining bias to the front of the mat, following the

curved corners and including the pocket edges neatly. Trim excess fabric at the corners, then fold the bias over to the back and slipstitch.

7. Roll up and tie with a bow.

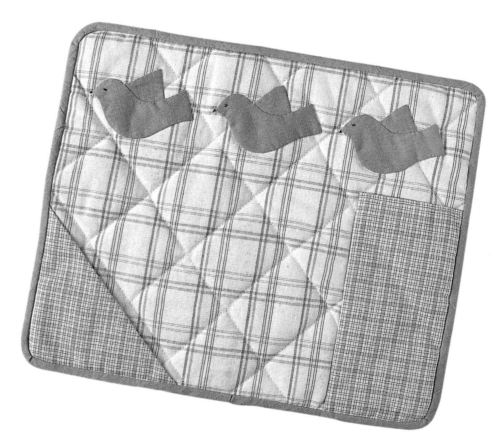

Cat Table Runner

SIZE 35 × 20 in/88.9 × 50.8 cm

MATERIALS

¾ yd/0.7 m backing
¾ yd/0.7 m wadding
¼ yd/0.25 m stripe for binding
½ yd/0.5 m cream for center
A fat quarter yd/m yellow for corner blocks
10 × 6 in/25 × 15 cm each of four cat fabrics
Scraps of beige, yellows, orange, rust, brown, grey, black and turquoise for the pieced blocks, and the remaining appliqués equivalent to ½ yd/0.5 m
Embroidery thread

METHOD

● Make templates for the appliqués as for the Goosegirl wallhanging.

● Cut a rectangle 24 × 9 in/ 61 × 22.8 cm for the center panel. Cut four blocks each 5½ × 5½ in/ 14 × 14 cm of yellow. From the turquoise cut two strips 1¼ × 25 in/3.2 × 63.5 cm; two strips 1¼ × 11½ in/3.2 × 29.2 cm.

Following directions for the Drunkard's Path border on the Goosegirl wallhanging, cut squares and circles for 56 units. Cut the appliqué motifs. For the binding, cut strips 1 in/2.5 cm wide totalling 114 in/290 cm.

● Appliqué the little houses and the egg basket. Sew the long framing strips of turquoise to the top and bottom of panel. Trim then complete with the side strips. Work the Drunkard's Path border units, and assemble into two sets of eight units for side borders and two sets of twenty units for top and bottom borders. Sew a corner block to both ends of each long border.

Join the side borders to the center panel. Work the cat motifs, leaving a gap when stitching the body for the tails. Add the lower border and the cat tails. Embroider the details using stem stitch. Attach the top border. Press, layer and quilt. Bind to finish.

Cowboy Quilt

While this quilt was being pieced I could not help wondering about all the young children, boys especially, who would be absolutely enthralled with it. This is a great adventure quilt. There are nine cowboys with whip in hand, galloping across the prairie rounding up the stray calf who is about to be set upon by an eagle and rattlesnake. This is an exciting project for all those quilters who are fascinated by the complexity of putting together many different fabrics.

SIZE 78 × 63½ in / 198 × 160 cm

MATERIALS

● Yardage requirements for the plaid fabrics only are based on 60 in/ 150 cm wide Mission Valley fabrics.

84 × 70 in / 213.4 × 177.8 cm backing

84 × 70 in / 213.4 × 177.8 cm wadding

¾ yd / 0.7 m red, black and beige plaid for binding

¾ yd / 0.7 m green/navy check for outer border

½ yd / 0.5 m beige check for middle border

¾ yd / 0.7 m dark browns for inner border and sashing strips

½ yd / 0.5 m each of three different plaids for framing the blocks

¼ yd / 0.25 m burgundy plain for pieced on-point setting squares plus an extra 16 × 2 in / 40.6 × 5 cm of peach for the odd blocks

25 × 2 in / 63 × 5 cm violet for centers

2 yd / 2 m mixed plaids, prints and plains, light and dark for the cowboy block backgrounds

Assorted squares for the post backgrounds: six 5 × 5 in / 12.7 × 12.7 cm, four 3½ × 3½ in / 9 × 9 cm corner squares and one 4 × 4 in / 10.2 × 10.2 cm appliqué setting square

Scraps for appliqué motifs

¾ yd / 0.7 m mixed plaids, prints and plains for the pieced blocks

Embroidery threads for features and details

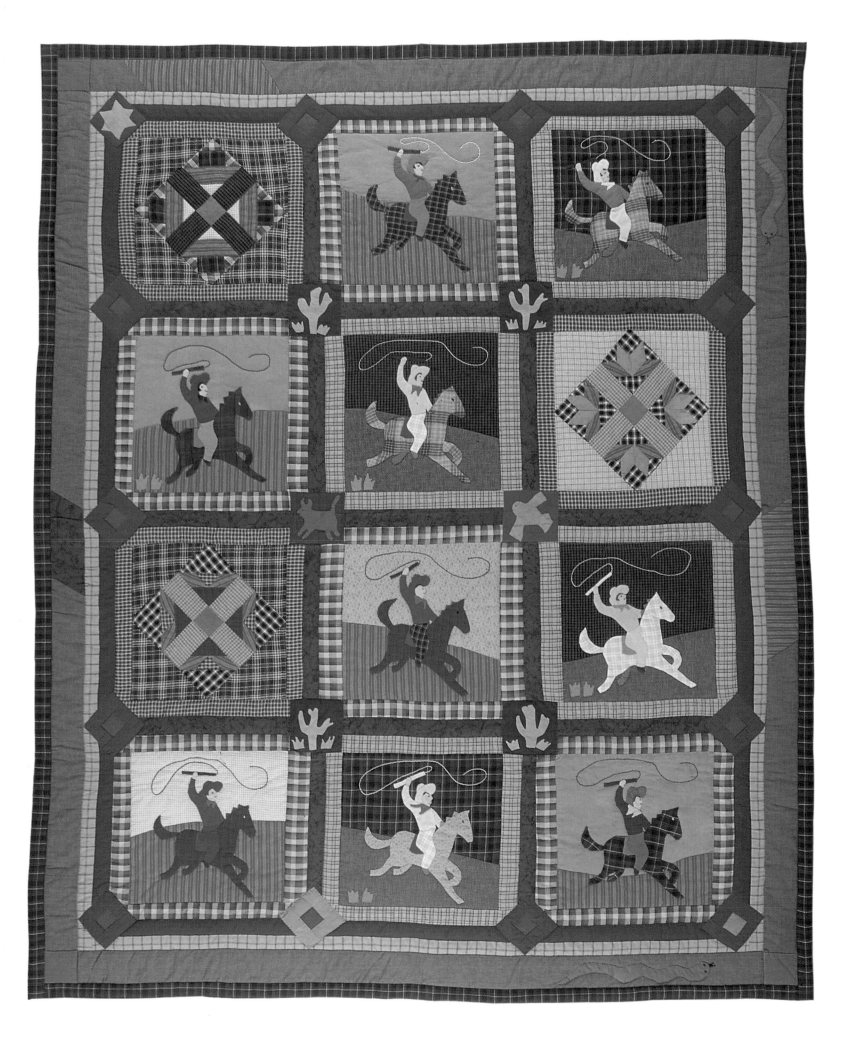

PATTERNS

Make templates for all the appliqué motifs and for the pieced blocks. Notice that the three pieced blocks are each slightly different.

CUTTING

1. From binding fabric cut six strips 3½ in/9 cm wide across the width of the fabric and set aside. From green/navy fine check cut the same, and label for outer border. From beige plaid cut six strips 1¾ in/ 4.5 cm wide for middle border. From dark browns cut eight strips 1¾ in/ 4.5 cm wide for inner border and sashing strips. From each of three framing fabrics cut four strips each 2 in/5 cm wide.

2. From the plain burgundy fabric cut four strips 1¾ in/4.5 cm wide across the fabric for the setting squares. Cut an assortment of backgrounds for the appliqué posts as listed in Materials.

3. Cut two fabrics each 14½ × 14½ in/36.8 × 36.8 cm and seam as necessary to make nine cowboy block backgrounds. This will allow for shrinkage due to the appliqué and possible fraying during handling. Follow the directions in the Ploughman wallhanging for sewing curved seams. Note that the horizon line flows between blocks at the same level.

4. Cut appliqué pieces for the cowboys, horses, cactus, calf, bird, snakes and star. The horses' manes can be made using prairie points as described in the Shepherd quilt, cutting three rectangles 1½ × 1 in/ 3.8 × 2.5 cm for each mane. Alternatively embroider the manes after completing the appliqué.

5. Cut out the shapes for one

pieced block. The remaining blocks will be cut at the sewing stage. To quick-cut the large corner triangles, cut two squares 7½ × 7½ in/19 × 19 cm in half diagonally. The four triangles will be slightly larger than required and will need trimming before framing.

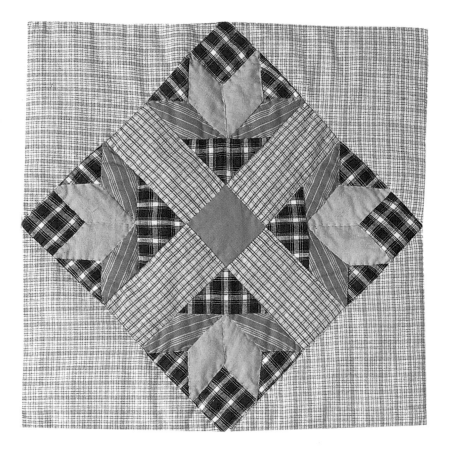

SEWING

1. Work all the appliqués except for the snakes. Prepare the prairie points for the horses' manes by pressing as described on page 66, then position them so that the top points sit correctly.

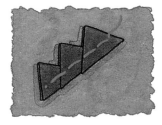

Use running stitches to hold the prairie points in position, just beneath the neck. Sew the neck in place, then before sewing further, lift the fabric and trim away the excess from the prairie points.

Embroider all the details. (The whips will be stitched during quilting.)

2. Make up the first pieced block using the design given, then cut out and piece two more variations.

3. Work the 13 on-point setting squares as directed on page 25 for the Chickengirl quilt, using the burgundy, peach and violet strips. Eleven blocks are burgundy with violet centers, one is burgundy with a peach center and one is peach with a violet center. Press under ¼ in/0.6 cm turning on all sides to prepare the setting squares for appliqué and set aside.

4. Trim the cowboy blocks to 13½ × 13½ in/34.3 × 34.3 cm, then add framing strips to the sides of the blocks only.

5. Press carefully, then lay out all the blocks, except for the on-point setting squares, in a pleasing arrangement. Sew framing strips to the tops of the three blocks in the top row. Press, then join these together alternating dark brown sashing strips in between blocks.

6. Piece the next row of framing strips sewn either side of dark brown sashing strips alternating with the appliqué posts.

Continue in this fashion until all the rows are sewn and press.

7. Join the rows together and add the dark brown inner border and beige middle borders, joining as required to make up the longer strips.

position, following the picture as a guide. Sew on the two side borders and press carefully. Next, sew a corner square to one end of each of the remaining shorter strips. Check against the quilt, adjusting the length before adding the remaining corner squares. Sew these borders to the top and bottom of the quilt and press.

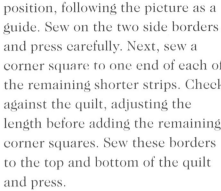

8. Appliqué the setting squares over the junctions, then trim away the patchwork from behind to reduce bulk.

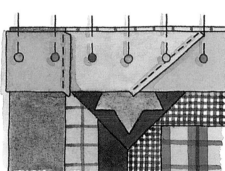

quilt like this, simply quilt in-the-ditch around the appliqué shapes and sashing strips, or echo quilt. A different emphasis can be given to the setting squares by quilting just inside the seams.

10. Embroider the whips.

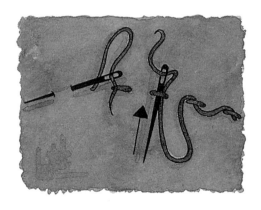

Sew strips together for the outer borders as required. After checking and adjusting the length of the side borders, appliqué the snakes in

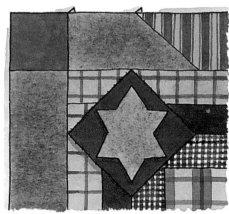

9. Press the top carefully and tidy the back. Spread the backing, RS down, with the wadding and quilt top RS up, on a flat surface. Pin or tack the layers together. On a busy

11. Trim excess backing and wadding to 1¼ in/3.2 cm all around. Machine sew the binding to the front of the quilt, with the raw edge even with the quilt top and taking ¼ in/0.6 cm seam. Fold the binding to the back, turn under ¼ in/0.6 cm and hem in place to conceal the machine stitching.

Cowboy Cushion

SIZE 15 × 15 in / 38 × 38 cm

MATERIALS

½ yd / 0.5 m plaid for backing

16 × 16 in / 40.7 × 40.7 cm calico to line the front

16 × 16 in / 40.7 × 40.7 cm wadding

Scraps equivalent to ⅛ yd / 10 cm for prairie points

Scraps for the pieced background, equivalent to a fat quarter yd/m

Scraps for appliqué motifs

Embroidery thread for details

METHOD

● Make templates for the cowboy as printed for the Cowboy single quilt.

● For the cushion back, cut two pieces 10½ × 15½ in / 26.7 × 39.5 cm. The remaining fabric can be used for the prairie points or the appliqués.

Cut 40 rectangles each 2¼ × 1¼ in / 5.8 × 3.2 cm for the prairie points.

Cut the appliqué pieces for the cowboy and horse.

Cut 25 squares each 3½ × 3½ in / 8.9 × 8.9 cm.

● Sew the 3½ in / 8.9 cm squares into five rows of five squares, pressing the seams in opposite directions on neighboring rows. Join the rows to complete the cushion background.

On the pieced background work the appliqué as directed in the

Cowboy quilt.

Embroider the details using three strands of thread.

Press, layer and quilt. Outline quilt around the horse and cowboy.

Trim wadding from the seam allowances.

Prepare the prairie points as in the Shepherd quilt. Arrange the points around the cushion front, raw edges level with the edge of the front and points facing into the middle of the cushion. There should be two points per background patch

and they should overlap slightly within the seam allowance. Machine-tack within the seam allowance using a long stitch.

Hem the cushion back panels as instructed in the Dancing Dog cushion on page 39.

Lay the two backs over the prepared front, RS facing the front and with the raw edges level with the edge of the front. Machine stitch all around the cushion, then turn to the right side, flipping the points out, and press the edges lightly.

Patchwork Cushion

SIZE 16 × 16 in/40.5 × 40.5 cm

MATERIALS

½ yd/0.5 m cushion backing

18 × 18 in/46 × 46 cm lining

18 × 18 in/46 × 46 cm wadding

2 strips each 12½ × 4½ in/32 × 11.5 cm of teal blue stripe

Scraps, none of which need be larger than a 6 in/15 cm square, for the pieced and appliqué blocks

¼ yd/0.25 m for binding

2 skeins stranded embroidery thread for tassels (each skein makes two tassels), or four purchased tassels

METHOD

● Make templates as directed in the Marriage quilt for the heart, flower and star.

● For the back cut two pieces each 16½ × 11 in/42 × 28 cm.

　For the binding, cut straightgrain strips 2 in/5 cm wide to total 68 in/ 172 cm.

　From scraps cut three squares each 4½ × 4½ in/11.4 × 11.4 cm for the appliqué background.

　Cut four hearts, two stars, a flower, three large and two small centers.

● Following the instructions in the Marriage quilt, make seven hourglass blocks.

　Work two strips of appliquéd hearts and the three little appliqué

blocks. Assemble as directed for one corner of the inner border, adding a heart setting strip to one side of the nine-patch unit. Sew the star appliqué block to the end of the remaining setting strip before attaching this to complete the cushion front.

　Layer, quilt and complete the cushion as directed in the Dancing Dog cushion project on page 39.

　To make quick tassels, from each skein of embroidery thread take 24 in/61 cm of thread, then lay the

skein on a flat surface. About ½ in/1.2 cm from both ends, bind around the skein with the length of thread just removed. Tie off very tightly, using a needle to hide the tails inside the tassel. One length should bind both ends of the skein. Cut the skein halfway between the two bindings to separate the two tassels.

　Secure one tassel to each corner of the cushion. This design would also look very good with a prairie point edging.

Shepherd Quilt

This is a beautifully designed but simple pictorial quilt that will be at its best when displayed on

a bed. It is divided into ten large blocks each with a single large motif that surround

the larger central medallion. These picture blocks are supported by a large landscape panel which

runs the width of the quilt and is designed to fall as a valance at the foot of

the bed. With its soft coloring, this quilt truly captures an English pastoral atmosphere.

SIZE 83 × 66 in / 210.8 × 167.6 cm

MATERIALS

● Yardage requirements for the plaid fabrics only are based on 60 in / 150 cm wide Mission Valley fabrics.

90 × 72 in / 228.6 × 182.9 cm calico for backing

90 × 72 in / 228.6 × 182.9 cm wadding

½ yd / 0.5 m pink and blue plaid for outer border

1 yd / 1 m fine blue and white plaid for sashing strips

¼ yd / 0.25 m black for hooves

Five assorted pale plaids for block backgrounds equivalent to 2 yd / 2 m in total

¼ yd / 0.25 m black and cream plaid for shepherd's suit

Scraps of beige, brown and white for face, hands, hair, collar and shoes

Scraps of green, tan, grey and beige for the owl

¼ yd / 0.25 m blue and white plaid for the hills

Nine scraps 8½ × 5 in / 21.5 × 12.7 cm of blue/white and black/white plaids for sheep

¼ yd / 0.25 m each of green for foliage, peach for sunset and wheat sheaves, brown for earth

Scraps of greens for tree trunks

¼ yd / 0.25 m each of blue, yellow and old gold for nine-patch and four-patch blocks

Embroidery thread for details

PATTERNS

Make templates for the shepherd, landscape, owl and sheep. For variety and ease of sewing, the hooves can be made using prairie points; however, this technique is suitable for hand-sewing, not for bonded appliqué. The templates for the ears and tail are very small: if you are less experienced at appliqué these can be embroidered instead.

CUTTING

1. From the pink and blue plaid cut six strips 3 in/7.5 cm wide across the full width of the fabric.

2. From the fine blue and white plaid cut one strip 2¼ × 60 in/ 5.7 × 152.4 cm, fourteen strips 2¼ × 19 in/5.7 × 48.3 cm, sixteen strips 2¼ × 15 in/5.7 × 38 cm and two strips 2¼ × 12 in/5.7 × 30.5 cm for the sashing.

3. From the pale plaids, cut one rectangle 59 × 12 in/149.8 × 30.5 cm for the landscape background, one rectangle 31 × 19 in/78.7 × 48.3 cm for the shepherd, and ten rectangles each 19 × 15 in/48.3 × 38 cm for the sheep and owl blocks.

4. Decide on your method of appliqué, then cut the pieces for the figure, landscape, owl and sheep.

5. For prairie point hooves cut 36 rectangles each 2 × 1¼ in/5 × 3.2 cm from the black fabric.

6. To strip-cut the nine-patch blocks, cut all strips 1¼ in/3.2 cm wide. From both the blue and the yellow, cut one strip 56 in/142.2 cm and two strips 30 in/76.2 cm. From the gold cut one strip 56 in/ 142.2 cm.

7. For the four-patch corner posts, cut a strip 16 × 1¾ in/40.5 × 4.5 cm from each of the yellow and the gold fabrics.

SEWING

1. Work the appliqué in your chosen method.

2. To make prairie point hooves, press under ¼ in/0.6 cm along one long edge of each black rectangle. Fold down the top left and right corners to meet in the center.

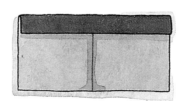

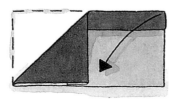

Fold this arrowhead shape in half to make a smaller triangle. Keep all edges and corners matching to ensure crisp points.

Tuck two triangles close together under the lower edge of each sheep as you appliqué the body. Catch the point of each triangle to the background with several "invisible" stitches.

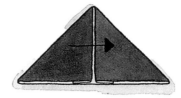

Complete each of the blocks by embroidering the details. Use small buttons for the shepherd's coat.

3. To quick-piece the four-patch corner posts sew together the 1¾ in/4.5 cm strips of yellow and gold down one long side. Press, then cross-cut into eight slices 1¾ in/

4.5 cm. Sew these slices together in pairs reversing one of each pair to produce the correct pattern.

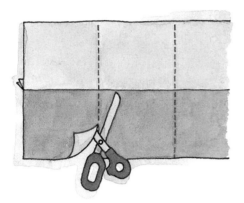

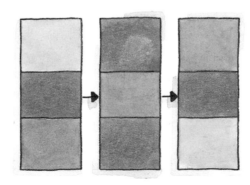

4. Using the 1¼ in/3.2 cm strips in a similar manner, quick-piece the nine-patch blocks. Make up one set, using the longest strips, of yellow, blue and gold. Press carefully, then cross-cut into 44 slices (two for each block) each 1¼ in/3.2 cm wide. Make up another set of one gold strip between two blue ones using the shorter lengths. Press the

strips carefully, then cut as before into 22 slices each 1¼ in/3.2 cm wide.

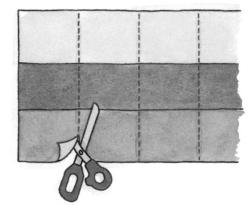

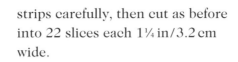

5. Pin, then sew the slices together in the correct pattern to make 22 nine-patch blocks.

6. When all the parts are finished, lay them out following the quilt as a

guide. Sew together in horizontal rows beginning with the top row of nine-patch blocks and sashing strips. Sew part rows and join these one above the other before sewing to each side of the central panel.

7. Measure across the center of the quilt top both vertically and horizontally to check the required lengths for the borders and make these up by joining the blue and pink plaid strips as necessary. Sew a four-patch corner post to both ends of the top and bottom borders.

8. Prepare the outside edges for finishing by pressing under a ¼ in/ 0.6 cm turning, along one side of each border. Attach side borders, press, then add the top and bottom borders. Complete the turn-under across the ends of these strips.

9. Press the quilt top carefully. Remove any loose threads. Spread the backing fabric, RS down, on a flat surface with the wadding over it. Center the quilt top over these, then pin and tack. Outline quilt around the appliqué shapes, blocks and border.

10. Trim excess wadding to the same size as the top. Leaving a ½ in/1.3 cm turning allowance trim the backing. Fold this turning over the wadding level with the quilt top, then sew the edges together. Top-stitch through all layers either by hand or machine. If you choose hand-sewing, add another row of quilting close to the edge to hold the wadding in place.

Grazing Sheep Table Runner

This simple to make table runner uses the sheep from the Shepherd quilt. The picture is framed with small pieced and appliqué blocks in the side borders and there are random strips of patchwork at the top and bottom. The beauty of this project lies in its inventive quilting.

SIZE 36 × 18 in/91.5 × 45.5 cm

MATERIALS

⅝ yd/0.6 m backing

⅝ yd/0.6 m low-loft or needle-punched wadding

½ yd/0.5 m pale plaid for center panel

¼ yd/0.25 m dark plaid for binding

⅛ yd/0.1 m black and white plaid for sheep

Assorted scraps for patchwork and appliqué, including solid black and white for faces

Embroidery threads for blanket stitching sheep and their features

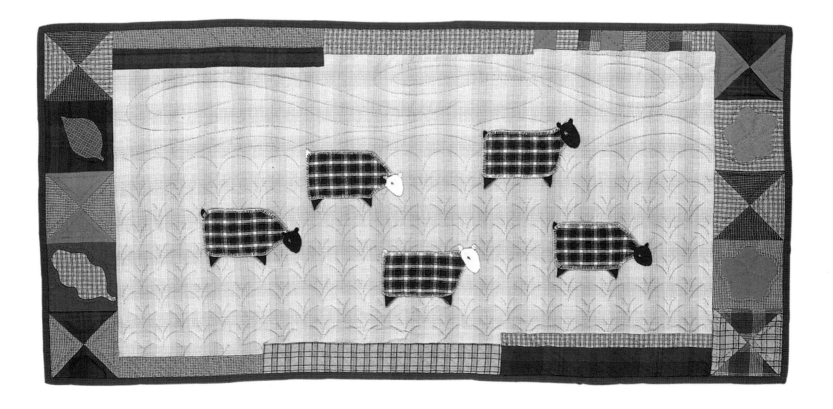

PATTERNS

Using the standing and grazing sheep from the Shepherd quilt make templates to measure 4 in /10 cm from nose to rear, not including the tail. Cut the template for the head without ears and embroider them instead. For the border appliqués, choose motifs from any of the designs in the book.

CUTTING

1. From the pale plaid cut a center panel 30 × 16 in/76.2 × 40.5 cm. From both wadding and backing cut a piece 38 × 20 in/96.5 × 51 cm.

2. Cut five bodies from the black and white plaid. Cut five heads, some from black and some from white solid fabric.

3. Cut ten rectangles of black or white each 1½ × 1 in/3.8 × 2.5 cm to make the hooves using the prairie point technique.

4. From dark plaid cut strips on the straight grain 1⅝ in/4 cm wide and totalling 3⅓ yd/3.2 m for the double binding.

5. For the side borders you will need ten small blocks. Decide how many of these will be appliqué and how many pieced. To make the hourglass blocks, cut squares 4¾ × 4¾ in/12 × 12 cm. For the appliqué blocks cut squares 4 × 4 in/10 × 10 cm. Cut the appliqué motifs as required.

SEWING

1. Tack the turnings under around the bodies, except where the head will overlap.

2. For the hooves, press under ¼ in/0.6 cm along one long side of each rectangle, fold lightly in half to find the center then fold the top right and left corners to meet in the center at the lower edge. Now fold in half again to enclose the previous layers.

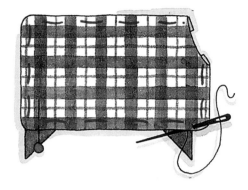

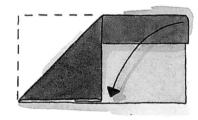

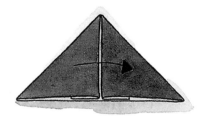

3. Position one triangle at the front and back of the body and slipstitch in place.

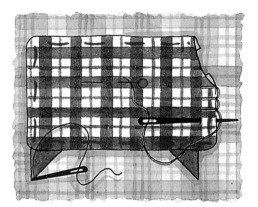

4. Arrange the sheep on the background and sew in place with blanket stitch.

5. Add the heads and attach the point of each foot with a small stitch. Embroider the ears, eyes and tails using satin stitch and French knots.

6. From scraps cut various strips and attach randomly to the top and bottom of the panel to measure 18 in/45.5 cm high. The first strip or two can be laid over the existing background if you wish to avoid having all strips beginning in a straight line. Some of the additional strips can be made up of small pieces.

7. Work the appliqué blocks for the borders using your chosen method, then work the pieced blocks. To work two hourglass blocks at a time, mark a 5¼ in/13.4 cm square with one diagonal on the WS of a piece of fabric. Place this RS together with a second fabric and sew ¼ in/0.6 cm away from both sides of the diagonal. Cut along all drawn lines through both layers and press, usually towards the darker fabric.

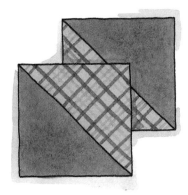

Mark the missing diagonal on the WS of one of the units. Place the two units RS together, with the colours opposite, and sew both sides of the marked diagonal. Cut between the lines of stitching and then press.

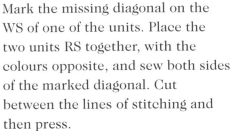

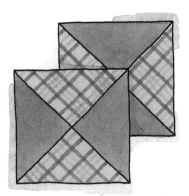

Make ten blocks. Join into two sets of five blocks and attach them to the sides of the center panel.

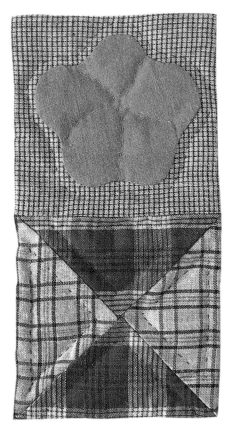

8. Press carefully, then mark the quilting design on the center panel. Mark the echo-quilting on the side blocks using ¼ in/0.6 cm masking tape as a guide.

9. Place the backing, RS down, on a flat surface, center the wadding and panel on top. Pin and tack the layers together, then quilt. Trim all the edges even, check that all corners are square.

10. Join the strips cut for the binding into a continuous length. Press the seams open, then press the binding in half along its length. Use this to bind the edges of the runner following the instructions for binding as given in the General Techniques chapter.

Farmyard Playmat

Starring a collection of animals from several of the larger quilt projects, our playmat is full of fun and very easy to make. Newcomers to quilting or those in a hurry for a gift can simply tie the quilt layers together. As the baby grows this can become a wallhanging for teaching names of animals.

SIZE   42½ × 42½ in / 108 × 108 cm

MATERIALS

1¼ yd / 1.15 m plaid for backing

1¼ yd / 1.15 m medium plaid for sashing

45 × 45 in / 114.3 × 114.3 cm wadding

¼ yd / 0.25 m each of four light or medium light plaids or stripes for block backgrounds

6 in / 15.2 cm squares of 16 different bright or light plaids, prints or plains for animals

1 yd / 1m paper-backed fusible web

Machine embroidery thread for appliqué

Embroidery thread for tying

PATTERNS

Make templates for the eight animals to fit a 6 in / 15.2 cm square. Each animal appears twice – once as is, and once reversed. Use the cockerel from the Dancing Couples wallhanging, the feeding hen and the fox from the Chickengirl quilt, the dog from the Apple Picker quilt, the cat and the goose from the Goosegirl wallhanging, the sheep from the Shepherd quilt and the pig from the Swineherd quilt.

CUTTING

1. From the medium plaid cut two strips 45 × 6¼ in / 114.3 × 16 cm and two strips 33½ × 6¼ in / 85 × 16 cm for the borders. Cut three strips 33½ × 3½ in / 85 × 9 cm and twelve strips each 6½ × 3½ in / 16.5 × 9 cm for the sashing.

2. From each of the four block background fabrics, cut four squares 6½ × 6½ in / 16.5 × 16.5 cm.

3. Onto the paper side of the fusible web, trace two of each animal remembering to reverse one. Cut out and bond to the WS of your chosen fabrics for the animals. Cut out again on the pencil line.

Use the remaining fabric for the feet, beaks and tails. Note that the cat's tail is a separate piece.

SEWING

1. Arrange the bonded shapes onto the block backgrounds and fuse following the manufacturer's directions. Machine zigzag around the shapes in matching or contrasting threads. Alternatively hand sew with blanket stitch.

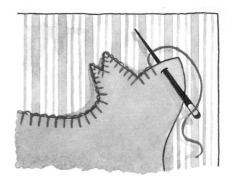

Embroider all the details by machine or by hand.

2. Lay the blocks out in a pleasing arrangement. Sew together in horizontal rows with the short sashing strips between the blocks.

Join the rows with the longer sashing strips.

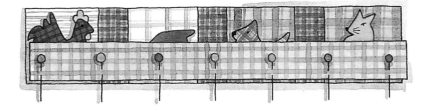

Add the shorter borders to the vertical sides of the mat and press. Sew the long borders to the top and bottom.

3. Press the top carefully and trim away any loose threads that may show through to the front. Spread out the backing RS down on a flat surface. Center the wadding and quilt top on the backing. Pin or tack the layers together. Tie with square knots at the corners of the blocks. See page 51 for diagrams and instructions for tying square knots. Outline quilt the animals and blocks. Quilt the border with concentric lines, using the lines of the plaid as a guide.

4. Trim the wadding and backing to 1 in / 2.5 cm smaller than the quilt top. Fold the border fabric over to the back, turn under ¼ in / 0.6 cm and slipstitch to finish.

Goosegirl Wallhanging

This wallhanging is a must for all those quilters who have often thought about wandering off
the "straight and narrow," going against convention, and who would like to take on the challenge of
sewing "crooked" seams. The central panel of the Goosegirl spills into the Drunkard's Path
border giving the wallhanging its informal and lively appearance. The same exuberance is expressed in
the crooked right-hand border where the seams wander in a delightfully irregular way. This
haphazard appearance can be captured by cutting the strips for the Drunkard's Path border freehand.

SIZE 37 × 33½ in / 94 × 85 cm approx.

MATERIALS

●Yardage requirements for the plaid
fabrics only are based on 60 in/
150 cm wide Mission Valley fabrics.
1¼ yd / 1.15 m backing
42 × 39 in / 106.5 × 99 cm wadding
¼ yd / 0.25 m bold plaid for binding
and inner frame
½ yd / 0.5 m lower background plaid

½ yd / 0.5 m medium dark plaid for
outer border and setting strips
¼ yd / 0.25 m each of two rust plaids
for clothing, brown plaid for hat and
baskets, three further background
plaids, black with rust plaid, plain
rust and white-on-calico

Small amounts of tea-dyed or beige
for corner block backgrounds, face
and hands. Navy for the corner posts.
Yellow for feet and bills. Peach,
yellow, grey, grey-green and mid
brown plains for quarter circles and
appliqués, plus assorted plaids and
prints for the Drunkard's Path blocks
Embroidery threads for details

PATTERNS

Make templates of all the motifs to suit your appliqué method, and also a template for the circle of the Drunkard's Path blocks. If available, cut twenty freezer paper circles to prepare the corner circles. For the landscape background make a full-size sketch on lightweight paper or muslin, 23¼ × 20 in/59 × 51 cm, following the illustration as a guide. Use the sketch as a foundation on which to sew the landscape.

CUTTING

1. From binding plaid cut four strips 1¼ in/3.2 cm wide and sew together to make a continuous binding. Also cut two strips 24 × 1 in/61 × 2.5 cm and two strips 21 × 1 in/53.3 × 2.5 cm for the inner frame around the center panel.

2. From the outer border fabric cut two strips 34½ × 3 in/87.5 × 7.5 cm and two strips 32 × 3 in /81 × 7.5 cm. Cut eight sashing strips 5½ × 3 in/ 14 × 7.5 cm which will be used to compensate for border variations. Cut four squares 3 × 3 in/7.5 × 7.5 cm for the corner posts.

3. Cut four squares 5½ × 5½ in/ 14 × 14 cm of tea-dyed or beige fabric for the corner block backgrounds. Cut the hand and face from the same fabric, then use the leftovers in the pieced border.

4. Cut the appliqué shapes using the illustration as a guide for choice and placement of colors.

5. From assorted fabrics cut 58 squares 3 × 3 in/7.5 × 7.5 cm for the pieced Drunkard's Path border. Iron the freezer paper circles to the WS of plain rust, peach, yellow, grey, mid brown and grey-green fabric and cut 20 circles adding ¼ in/ 0.6 cm turning by eye as you cut.
● If you choose not to taper the theme panel, cut two further 3 in/ 7.5 cm squares.

SEWING

1. Following the method given for sewing the background of the Apple Picker quilt, work the background for the center panel over the sketched foundation.

2. Work the corner blocks and the center panel except for the front goose. As there are dark fabrics in this design, trim layers from behind appliqué shapes as you go. Embroider the details. To taper the panel, trim the right-hand side by 3¼ in/8.3 cm from the lower right corner, tapering off near the top.

3. Sew the narrow inner framing strips to the center panel.

4. To make the Drunkard's Path blocks, first gather the circles over the freezer paper and press with a little spray-starch. Ease out the papers and cut the fabric circles into quarters.

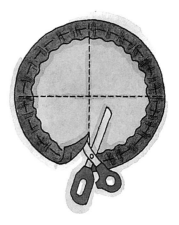

Position a quarter-circle over a corner of a 3 in/7.5 cm square and using the blindhem stitch on the machine with matching thread, sew in place.

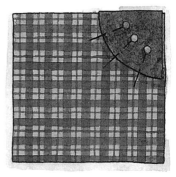

5. Trim away the fabric from behind the applied corner to reduce bulk, being careful not to pierce the top layer.

Repeat as necessary adding quarter-circles in a random way to the blocks, varying placement and number applied. Follow our hanging or use your own preferences when arranging the blocks.

6. Assemble the blocks into borders of two rows of blocks.

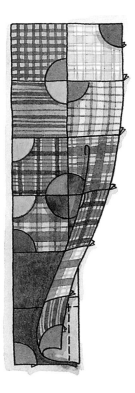

Make two sets of 16 blocks for the sides, one set of 14 for the top and a set of 12 for the bottom. Sew a sashing strip to each end of all border strips.

7. Join the side borders to the framed center, trimming the sashing strips as necessary. Press. Appliqué the front goose.

8. Check the lengths of the top and bottom borders, trimming the sashing strips as required before sewing a corner appliqué block to the ends of both borders. Attach these borders, then appliqué the cat in position on the border.

9. Sew an outer border strip to each side of the quilt, trimming if

needed. Press, then check the required length of the top and bottom outer borders before sewing on the navy corner posts and attaching these borders to the quilt.

10. Press the top carefully and trim away any loose threads that may show to the front. Lay the backing RS down, the wadding and the top, RS up, on a flat surface, then pin and tack the layers together. Outline quilt the appliqué motifs, and add extra lines to suggest clouds and sunrays. Use blanket stitch around the geese for added texture.

11. Using the prepared binding strips finish the wallhanging with separate binding as directed in the General Techniques chapter.

Goose Chase Tablecloth

Using the wreath from the Marriage Quilt and an enlarged version of the front goose from the Goosegirl wallhanging, this appealing tablecloth can be completed in a relatively short time. The color scheme is simple, and choosing bold plaids for the geese instead of a more predictable white creates unexpected interest and adds a festive touch to the finished article. Alternatively, this design could be worked into a stylish throw by raising the appliqué with wadding, then layering the top to finish in the standard way.

SIZE 50 × 50 in / 127 × 127 cm

MATERIALS

1½ yd / 1.5 m fine light colored plaid for cloth

½ yd / 0.5 m each of two red plaids for geese

Scraps of gold for feet and bills, green for leaves, crimson for flowers and yellow for centers

Black embroidery thread

PATTERNS

Make templates for the wreath and goose. The wreath is exactly the same size as used in the Marriage Quilt. The goose is the front goose from the Goosegirl wallhanging. It should measure 10½ in / 26.7 cm from the top curve of the neck to the feet.

CUTTING

1. Cut a square of the light plaid measuring 52 × 52 in/132 × 132 cm.

2. For the appliqués, cut eight geese, four from each of the two plaids, eight sets of bills and feet from the gold fabric, twenty green leaves, four crimson flowers and four flower centers.

SEWING

1. Press a 1 in/2.5 cm turning to the WS of the light plaid for a hem. Turn under the raw edge again and sew in place by hand or machine, or using an embroidery stitch.

2. Fold the cloth in half both ways to find the center then place the wreath pattern underneath and lightly mark some parts of the design for placement guidelines.

Appliqué the wreath, tucking one leaf behind each flower.

Add a center to each flower.

3. Position the geese around the wreath, placing one centrally on each side then the remaining four in between. Fold the cloth diagonally for placement, carefully avoiding stretching the fabric.

Tack the body in position while you apply the bill and feet, or you can start sewing the body and add the feet and bill as you reach them. Embroider the eyes on the geese with satin stitch or a French knot.

Café Curtain

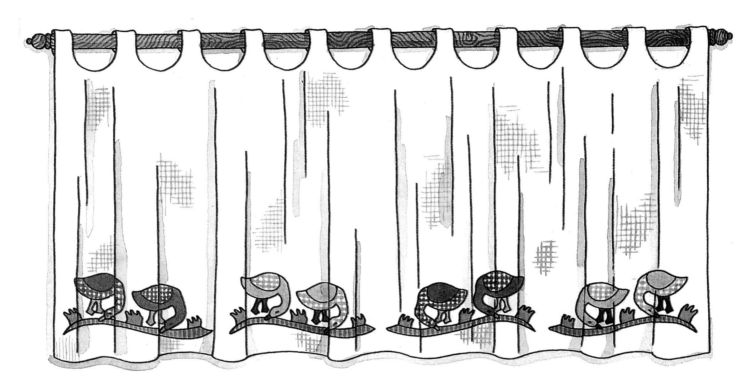

SIZE Measure to fit your own window. This café-style curtain does not need to be very full, but add approx. 18 in/ 46 cm to the length for finishing the top and the hem.

MATERIALS

Curtain fabric, quantity as determined above
Scraps of plains, plaids and stripes for the geese appliqués

METHOD

● Make templates for the geese used in the the Ploughman wallhanging. Make a card template for marking the top of the curtain. See page 143 in the Template Section.

● Using the templates, cut out the geese, noting that two face one way and two the other. You may need to vary the number of repeats to suit the size of your window.

Trim your curtain fabric to a true rectangle, if necessary.

● Press and sew a narrow hem on the sides of the curtain. Turn under and sew a hem across the top edge. From this finished edge across the width of the curtain, measure 7 in/17.8 cm to mark where to fold the top over to become the self-facing, see marking template. Fix the spacing between the U-shapes to give a whole number of repeats, keeping the spacing consistent across the curtain. Place the marking template on the WS of the curtain at the top and mark out for sewing the curves.

After marking, carefully fold the self-facing over at the top RS together and sew around each of the U-shapes. Trim away the inside of the U, leaving ¼ in/0.6 cm seam allowance. Clip the curves. Turn RS out, pushing the top corners out carefully.

Fold over the finished straps and sew in place, either invisibly to the facing or by machine through all the layers. Slipstitch the self-facing and curtain together at the sides.

Press a double 2 in/5 cm hem at the bottom and sew in place. Work the appliqué geese motifs along the bottom edge of the curtain.

Blacksmith's Boy Cot Quilt

This small quilt or wallhanging can be worked in a piecemeal way. Working one area at a time in this manner, it is not essential that you follow the color choices or even the patchwork or appliqué. Provided that all the sections finally fit together, you can choose motifs and block designs from other projects in the book. This is a very satisfying project for lovers of scrap quilts. Instructions are given for the example shown but once started I am certain that you will find inspiration from the particular fabrics being used at the time.

SIZE 39 × 38½ in/99.1 × 97.8 cm

MATERIALS

45 × 48 in/114 × 122 cm backing

42 × 42 in/106.7 × 106.7 cm wadding

½ yd/0.5 m assorted blue plaids for borders and corner posts

¼ yd/0.25 m green plaid for leaf-block backgrounds

Mixed remnants, none greater than 18 in/45.7 cm for block backgrounds

Scraps for appliqué shapes and small pieced units

Embroidery threads

PATTERNS

Make templates for the boy, the dog and the horseshoe. Make templates for both versions of the sheep from the Shepherd quilt, adjusting the pattern to measure 4 in/10 cm from nose to tail. To make the hooves using prairie points refer to the instructions in the Shepherd quilt, but use rectangles 1 × 1½ in/ 2.5 × 3.8 cm.

CUTTING

1. From the darkest blue border plaids, cut four squares 3 × 3 in/ 7.5 × 7.5 cm for the corner posts. From the second darkest cut four strips 1½ × 4 in/3.8 × 10.2 cm and four strips 1½ × 3 in/3.8 × 7.5 cm. Cut enough strips from the remaining blues 3½ in/8.9 cm wide to make up four borders each at least 34 in/86.4 cm long.

2. For the leaf blocks cut two rectangles 18 × 8½ in/45.7 × 21.5 cm from the green plaid. From the remnants, cut block backgrounds to the following sizes:
boy 16 × 12¾ in /40.6 × 32.4 cm
sheep 18 × 9¼ in/45.7 × 23.5 cm
horseshoes 6¼ × 17 in/16 × 43.2 cm
dog A 8½ × 8¾ in/21.5 × 22.2 cm
dog B 10¾ × 7¼ in/27.3 × 18.5 cm
flowers 8¼ × 6½ in/21 × 16.5 cm.
For additional variety you may prefer to piece some of the blocks from two or more different fabrics.

3. For the four-patch blocks, cut two squares 5 × 5 in/12.7 × 12.7 cm of light blue plaid. From assorted scraps, cut ten 2 in/5.1 cm squares, a strip 2 × 5 in/5.1 × 12.7 cm, three squares 2⅜ × 2⅜ in/6 × 6 cm to be divided once diagonally and some

smaller squares 1¼ in /3.2 cm as required to fill.

4. From available scraps cut the appliqué pieces for the boy, three horseshoes, three sheep and two dogs. For the leaf blocks, cut six bias strips 8 × ¾ in/20.3 × 2 cm. Cut 42 leaves freehand, roughly in a diamond shape, 2½ in/6.5 cm from point to point. Also freehand cut two flowers, each made up of three layers and a center.

5. You will need to cut a few "filler" rectangles but this is best done when the appliqué blocks have been worked and it will be possible to check the exact sizes required for your quilt.

SEWING

1. Work the appliqué blocks first. The illustration shows trapunto or stuffed appliqué for the sheep, the flowers and the boy's arm and leg. Insert a little wadding with an orange stick before finally sewing down the last edge of the shape.

On the leaf blocks, lightly draw or tack the line of the stem, then apply the leaves. Press the bias strips into thirds down the length, position each one over a marked line and blindhem in place.

Embroider the details except the whip. This will be done when all the blocks have been sewn together.

2. Following the illustration as a guide, make up the two pieced units for the four-patch block. Join with the 5 in/12.7 cm squares into a large four-patch block.

3. Lay out the blocks and determine the sizes needed for the filler rectangles. Cut these and join together. Some fillers are pieced – make your own decisions according to the fabrics available, then join all together. For help on dealing with inset corners see the instructions and illustrations for the Old Homestead quilt on pages 12–14.

4. Now embroider the whip: see the Cowboy quilt on page 61.

5. Assemble the border strips into four units. Sew the narrow strips to the four dark corner posts on two sides only.

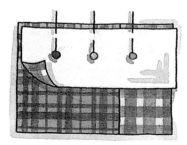

6. Join one of these to each end of two borders, being careful to position them correctly.

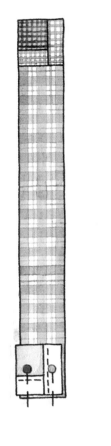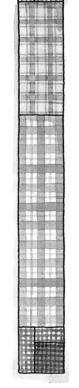

7. Sew the two shorter borders to the sides of the quilt. Press, then attach the top and bottom borders.

8. Press the quilt top carefully. Trim away any loose threads.

9. Lay the backing, RS down, on a flat surface with the wadding and top centered over it. Pin and tack the layers together.

10. Quilt the appliqués in-the-ditch or outline quilt just within the appliqué, close to the edge. Effective use can be made of the different

plaids for quilting designs of parallel lines, grids (not necessarily regular), diagonals and chevrons. Other ideas include castellations as used in the border and echo quilting, as used around the flowers. Play with the possibilities – for instance, an attractive surface is created on the lower dog by quilting very regular stitches in both directions on a ¼ in/0.6 cm plaid but this is contrasted by simply quilting the outline of the other dog. Do not feel that the same shape or fabric must be treated in the same way. Aim for about an equal amount of quilting over the entire quilt but make sure to vary the density from place to place. Do not quilt right to the edges before finishing them off.

11. Trim the wadding ¼ in/0.6 cm smaller than the quilt top and the backing ½ in/1.2 cm smaller than the top. Fold-finish as directed in the General Techniques chapter.

12. Complete working the quilting right to the finished edges.

Swineherd Quilt

This quilt was designed as a companion for the Shepherd quilt, and they do look wonderful

side by side. They share the same simple yet unusual layout and many of the

same fabrics. The simplicity of the design makes it a perfect vehicle for substituting the main motifs

with motifs of your choice. Do not be daunted by the idea of sewing two quilts.

Using such large blocks and simple shapes you will find that each project grows very quickly.

SIZE 88½ × 67 in / 224.8 × 170.2 cm

MATERIALS

● Yardage requirements for the plaid fabrics only are based on 60 in / 150 cm wide Mission Valley fabrics.

94 × 73 in / 238.8 × 185.4 cm calico for backing

94 × 73 in / 238.8 × 185.4 cm wadding

½ yd / 0.5 m pink and blue plaid for outer border

1 yd / 1 m fine blue and white plaid for sashing strips

Five assorted light plaids for block backgrounds

Nine scraps 12 × 7 in / 30.5 × 17.8 cm of peach, terracotta and red plaids for pigs and one piece 8 × 5 in / 20.3 × 13 cm of blue / white plaid for sheep

Two scraps 15 × 7 in / 38 × 17.8 cm of check or plain violet fabrics for blouse and skirt

Scraps of tan, old gold, geranium pink, brown, and peach for face, hands, hair, hat, stick, pantalettes and boots

Scraps of grey, grey-green, beige and off-white for the pigs' feet, sheep's face and feet, buckets and spilt milk

¼ yd / 0.25 m grey-violet for hills

¼ yd / 0.25 m each of terracotta for foliage, peach for ground, and two browns for tree trunks and shack

¼ yd / 0.25 m each of rust, grey and rose pink for nine-patch and four-patch blocks

Embroidery thread for features and details

PATTERNS

Enlarge the patterns for the swineherd, the landscape, the sheep and the pigs to the correct sizes and make templates for each. There are two different pigs, one smiling and the other glum. Both are used as given and in reverse. For visual variety and ease of sewing, the pigs' feet can be made like prairie points. This method is most suitable for hand sewing rather than bonded appliqué. The templates for the sheep ears and tail are small – if you are less experienced at appliqué these could be embroidered instead.

CUTTING

1. From the pink and blue plaid cut six strips 3 in/7.6 cm wide across the full width of the fabric.

2. From the fine blue and white plaid cut one strip 2¾ × 60 in/7 × 152.4 cm, fourteen strips 2¾ × 19 in/7 × 48.3 cm and eighteen strips 2¾ × 15 in/7 × 38 cm to make the sashing.

3. From light plaids, cut one rectangle 59½ × 15 in/151 × 38 cm for the landscape, one rectangle 31 × 18½ in/78.7 × 47 cm and ten rectangles each 18½ × 15 in/47 × 38 cm for the sheep and pig blocks.

4. From appropriate fabrics and using the method suited to your planned appliqué technique, cut the appliqué pieces for the Swineherd, landscape, pigs and sheep. Use the illustration as a guide. For prairie point pig feet cut 36 rectangles each 2 × 1¼ in/5 × 3.2 cm from the scraps of grey fabric.

5. Make the sheep's feet in the same way.

6. For the nine-patch blocks, cut all strips 1¼ in/3.2 cm wide. Cut four strips from each of the rust and grey fabrics 30 in/76.5 cm long. Cut one strip 30 in/76.5 cm long from the rose pink fabric.

7. For the four-patch corner posts, cut a strip 16 × 1¼ in/40.5 × 4.5 cm from each of the rust and rose pink fabric.

SEWING

1. Work the appliqué motifs following the directions in the General Techniques chapter for your chosen method.

To make prairie point feet for the pigs, see the instructions in the Shepherd quilt. Decorate the center panel with a small appliqué block.

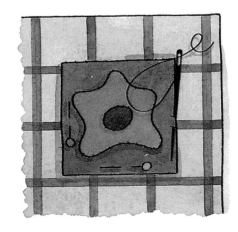

Also add an hourglass block worked from scraps. The instructions can be found in the Barnyard Placemats project on pages 92–3.

Complete the blocks by embroidering all the details.

2. Make the four-patch corner posts. Sew together the wider strips of rust and rose pink down one long side. Press then cross-cut into eight slices 1¾ in/4.5 cm.

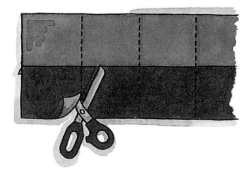

Sew these slices together in pairs, reversing one of each pair to produce the correct pattern.

3. Using the narrower strips in a similar manner, quick-piece the nine-patch blocks. Make up two sets of strips in the color combination of rust-grey-rust. Press, then cross-cut into 44 slices (two for each block) each 1¼ in/3.2 cm wide.

Make up another set of one rose pink strip between two grey ones. Cut across into 22 slices each 1¼ in/3.2 cm wide.

4. Pin, then sew slices together in the correct order to make 22 nine-patch blocks.

5. Lay out the parts following the quilt plan given below.

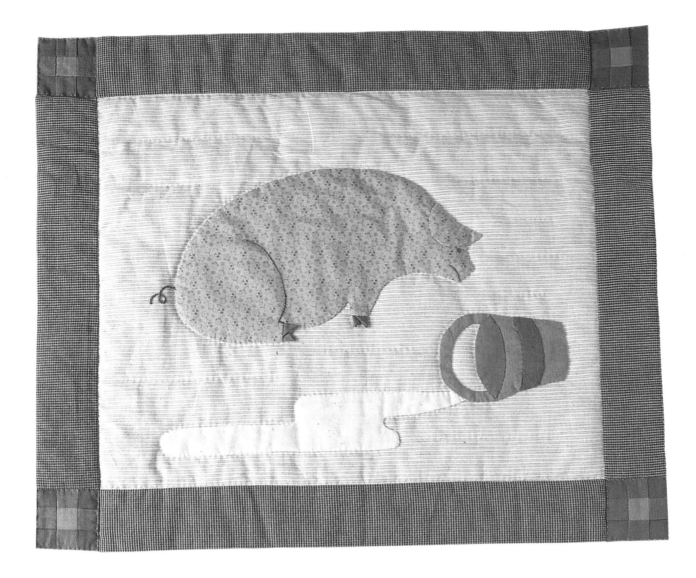

Assemble in horizontal rows beginning with the top row of nine-patch blocks and sashing strips. Sew part rows and join these one above the other before sewing to each side of the center panel.

6. Measure across the middle both vertically and horizontally to check the required lengths for the side, top and bottom borders and make these up by joining the blue and pink plaid strips as necessary. Sew a four-patch corner post to both ends of the top and bottom borders.

7. Prepare the outside edges for finishing by pressing under ¼ in/ 0.6 cm turning down one side of each border. Attach side borders and press. Then add the top and bottom borders. Complete the turn-under across the ends of these strips and tack.

8. Spread the backing fabric, RS down, on a flat surface with the wadding over it. Center the quilt top over these, then pin and tack.

9. Outline quilt around the

appliqué shapes, blocks and border. Additional quilting may be added to the block backgrounds by following some of the lines of the plaids.

10. Trim the excess wadding and backing ½ in/1.2 cm smaller than the prepared edge of the top. Fold this ½ in/1.2 cm turning over to the back of the quilt and sew the prepared edge in place.

11. If you wish, add another row of quilting close to the edge to hold the wadding in place.

Barnyard Placemats

Give your dining table a wholesome homespun look with these four randomly pieced placemats. You may want to add to the set by making further mats using motifs from other projects in the book.

SIZE 12½ × 9½ in/31.8 × 24 cm

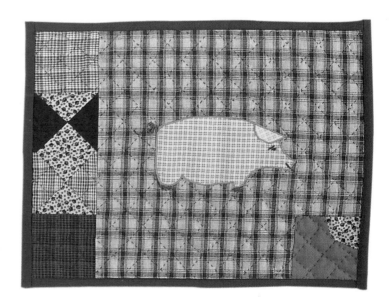

MATERIALS

½ yd/0.5 m assorted blue plaids, plains and prints

½ yd/0.5 m navy for binding and patchwork

½ yd/0.5 m backing

½ yd/0.5 m wadding

Scraps of peach, yellows and old golds for the appliqué motifs

¼ yd/0.25 m paper-backed fusible web

Machine embroidery threads

Embroidery thread for details

PATTERNS

Make templates for each animal to measure 5 in/12.7 cm across the greatest dimension. Our mats feature the cat and the corner goose from the Goosegirl wallhanging, the standing pig from the Swineherd quilt and the owl from the Shepherd quilt. You could substitute motifs from other projects in the book if you prefer. To decorate the mats with Drunkard's Path blocks make a card or freezer paper template of the circle supplied for the Goosegirl wallhanging.

CUTTING

1. From the backing and wadding cut four rectangles each 12½ × 9½ in/31.8 × 24 cm.

2. From assorted blues, cut four rectangles 10½ × 9½ in/26.7 × 24 cm for the appliqué background blocks. Cut six squares 3½ × 3½ in/ 9 × 9 cm and cut twice diagonally to

make hourglass blocks. Cut six squares 3⅜ × 3⅜ in/8.6 × 8.6 cm and cut in half diagonally. Cut six more squares 2¾ × 2¾ in/7 × 7 cm. For the Drunkard's Path blocks cut six squares 2¾ × 2¾ in/7 × 7 cm and three circles using the circle template, adding ¼ in/0.6 cm seam allowance as you cut.

3. Trace the animal shapes in reverse on the paper side of the fusible web. Cut out roughly, then bond to the WS of your chosen fabrics. Cut out carefully.

4. From the navy fabric cut 1 in/ 2.5 cm wide strips for binding. Each mat requires a minimum 48 in/ 122 cm of binding.

SEWING

1. For this project work the appliqué motifs using the bonded appliqué method.

2. First make templates for all motifs, then place them on the paper side of the fusible web, and carefully trace the shapes using a well-sharpened pencil.

3. Cut out, allowing a small margin all round.

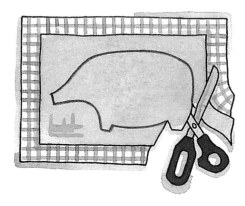

4. Fuse the webbing to the WS of the appliqué fabric.

5. When cold, cut out the shapes exactly on the pencil line and peel away paper backing.

6. Details can be embroidered by hand or machine depending on your skill level and preference.

7. Using the triangles cut, make up a few four-color pieced blocks for the side borders.

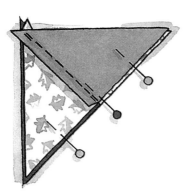

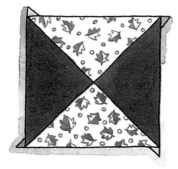

8. For variety, make up several two-color blocks using triangles already cut, following the illustrations below.

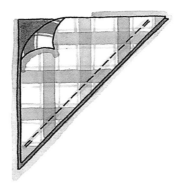

9. Assemble into sets of four with the plain squares. Make a pleasing arrangement, different for each mat.

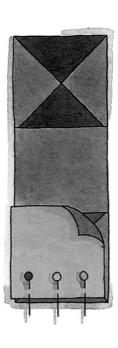

10. Make the Drunkard's Path blocks following the instructions in the Goosegirl wallhanging. Appliqué these here and there to the background rectangles, along with any other strips, by first pressing under a ¼ in/0.6 cm turning along two sides and then blindhemming to the background.

11. Attach one border to each mat.

12. For each mat assemble the backing, RS down, a rectangle of wadding and the prepared top, RS up. Pin and tack the layers together, then quilt in a diagonal grid, marked with masking tape.

13. Bind the mats to finish following instructions in the General Techniques chapter.

Ploughman Wallhanging

This small wallhanging incorporates many of the design elements used in the larger projects and it provides a good opportunity to practice some of the necessary skills. It offers an introduction to a technique of curved piecing invented by Marilyn Stothers and the short side borders are a good vehicle for practicing some of the various quick-piecing techniques which are essential for the narrow sawtooth outer border. The large open spaces are ideal to show off some inventive quilting. You may want to consider creating a country landscape. Look at the Grazing Sheep table runner and the Marriage quilt for inspiration.

SIZE   36½ × 26 in / 92.7 × 66 cm

MATERIALS

● Yardage requirements for the plaid fabrics only are based on 60 in / 150 cm wide Mission Valley fabrics.
¾ yd / 0.75 m backing
40 × 30 in / 101.5 × 76 cm wadding
¼ yd / 0.25 m dark plaid for binding

½ yd / 0.5 m each of dark brown and earth red for sawtooth border
¾ yd / 0.75 m light plaid for main background
¼ yd / 0.25 m light brown and light grey-green for curved piecing

Scraps of assorted plaids and plains for the appliqués and border including warm beige, black for hats and shoes, mauve for corner accent squares, green for grass and a second green strip for the curved piecing
Embroidery threads

PATTERNS

From the patterns provided, make templates for the ploughman, horse, geese and the little jug. To create the mirror image of the main motifs, reverse the templates.

CUTTING

1. From the dark plaid cut strips 1 in/2.5 cm wide to total 3⅝ yd/ 3.5 m for binding.

2. For the curved piecing begin by cutting rectangles of the appropriate fabrics as listed:
light plaid background two pieces each 29½ × 11 in/75 × 28 cm
light brown three strips each 29½ × 3 in/75 × 7.5 cm
light grey-green three strips each 29½ × 3 in/75 × 7.5 cm
second green one strip about 15 × 3 in/38.1 × 7.5 cm.
Note: the curves will be cut at the sewing stage.

3. From the assorted scraps cut the appliqué motifs for the central panel and for the border blocks.

4. Cut six squares 3½ × 3½ in/ 9 × 9 cm for border appliqué backgrounds from various plains or plaids, and four squares 1¼ × 1¼ in/ 3.2 × 3.2 cm of mauve for the outer border corners.

5. Cut each of the dark brown and earth-red fabrics into 13 rectangles 5 × 7 in/12.7 × 17.8 cm for quick-piecing the sawtooth border.

SEWING

1. Practice the curved piecing first on some spare fabric. To repeat the same curve each time cut out a paper guide. The edge of the paper guide marks your cutting line. The fabrics will be sewn with ¼ in/ 0.6 cm seams. Place the two edges which are to be sewn, RS up on top of each other with short ends even. Mark a curve using the paper guide previously mentioned, or freehand if preferred. If using a rotary cutter, a large cutting mat is essential to support the whole width of fabric. The two cut edges will automatically fit together so discard the smaller offcuts into your scrap bag.

Lay the fabrics, RS together, matching. Pin the raw edges and the curves. Sew the seam carefully then clip the curves before pressing the seams open.

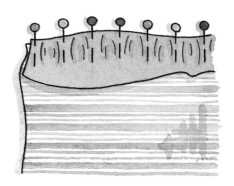

Following this technique, add a strip of light brown to both the top and lower edges of one light plaid background rectangle.

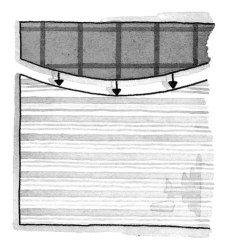

Add a strip of light brown to the lower edge of the second rectangle. Press, then sew a strip of green to the top of the background.

2. Work the main appliqués on these panels, centering the figure between the top and bottom seams. Also work the six little appliqué blocks for the borders. Embroider the details.

3. Join the top and lower panels using the curved seam technique. Measure the panel height as you add a strip of light grey-green to the top and lower edges. In our example, the top strip of green is neither visible across the whole width of the panel, nor at the bottom, though an extra short curved strip of a second green fabric was needed to maintain the curved design halfway along the lower edge. Your panel may not match the illustration exactly. Trim the center panel to measure 29 × 24½ in / 73.6 × 62.3 cm.

4. Piece nine hourglass blocks for the border following the method given in the Marriage Quilt. Join the pieced and appliqué border blocks into two sets of eight. Press, then sew to the vertical sides of the central panel.

5. To quick-piece the sawtooth border, mark out grids of six squares 2⅛ × 2⅛ in / 5.4 × 5.4 cm, on the wrong side of the earth-red fabric. Also mark one diagonal in each square ensuring that they run in opposite directions in neighboring squares. Lay the marked fabric, RS

together, with the dark brown and sew along both sides of all marked diagonals following the illustrations given below.

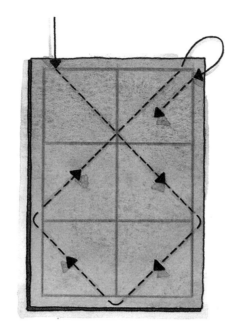

Next, cut along all marked lines and press the units open to give you your two-color squares.

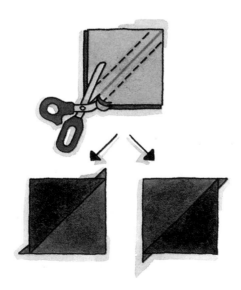

From each grid you will get twelve squares, each one made up of a dark brown and a red triangle.

6. Join the units into two strips of 44 squares and two strips of 30 squares, ensuring they face the same way to create the sawtooth pattern. You may need one or two squares more or less.

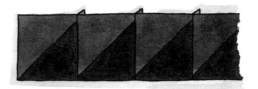

7. Attach the two vertical side outer borders and check the required length of the top and bottom borders by measuring across the middle of the quilt. Sew on an accent corner square at one end of the long sawtooth strips. Then mark the required length of the border and attach the remaining corner squares. Join the top and bottom borders to the quilt.

8. Press the top carefully. Trim away any loose threads. Place the backing RS down, center the wadding and top RS up, on a flat surface. Pin then tack the layers together. A machine embroidery pattern has been designed to suggest furrows in the background panels.

9. After quilting, bind the wallhanging using the separate binding method described in the General Techniques chapter.

10. Sew on a hanging sleeve if you intend to use this project as a wallhanging. Refer to the General Techniques chapter for instructions.

The Marriage Quilt

A jubilant combination of colors and motifs makes this a truly celebratory quilt. The center panel is

a warm and simply achieved image of the marriage couple. It is framed with a patchwork

of hourglass blocks and a sprinkling of naive appliqué motifs. A large number of different fabrics

have been included in the frame and it offers a great opportunity to include fabrics

with special associations for the happy couple. The border of the wedding procession is made up

of all the characters that appear in other projects in the book. They are

sewn as blocks, their backgrounds constructed from several shades of tea-dyed fabrics.

SIZE 87½ × 87in/222.3 × 221 cm

MATERIALS

● Yardage requirements for the plaid fabrics only are based on 60 in/ 150 cm wide Mission Valley fabrics.
94 × 94 in/239 × 239 cm backing
94 × 94 in/239 × 239 cm wadding
6 yd × 45 in wide/6 m × 114.3 cm wide calico for center panel and borders
1 yd/1 m soft red for binding

¼ yd/0.25 m burgundy for narrow border inside binding
½ yd/0.5 m terracotta stripe for heart setting strips, woman's dress and corner blocks
½ yd/0.5 m plain geranium pink, black and white-on-calico
¼ yd/0.25 m purple for framing the central panel

2 yd/2 m assorted scraps for the hourglass blocks, corner four-patches and small appliqué blocks in a mixture of plaids and plains.
1½ yd/1.5 m assorted plaid and plain scraps for the border appliqué. It is better to have small amounts of many fabrics than large amounts of a few.
Embroidery threads for details

PATTERNS

Make templates for all the patterns to suit your chosen method of appliqué. The wreath should measure 15 in/38 cm across.

CUTTING

1. From the background calico cut one piece 1½ yd /135 cm across the width of the fabric. From this piece the center panel will be cut. Divide the remaining calico into four equal parts. Set aside one of the four parts. Dye the rest, including the 1½ yd/135 cm piece in four shades of beige/brown according to the directions on page 104 in the General Techniques chapter. The 1½ yd /135 cm for the center should be dyed to the lightest shade.

2. From the lightest of the dyed fabrics cut the center panel 28 × 28 in/71 × 71 cm. Cut the rest of the dyed calico into strips 4½ in/ 11.5 cm wide. Leftovers will always be useful for small motifs such as

faces and hands and other small details. A few pieces can be used in the hourglass blocks to give that added little sparkle and contrast.

3. Cut four strips 1¼ × 20 in/ 3.2 × 50.8 cm each of geranium pink and purple for framing the center panel. Cut an extra two strips the same size in geranium pink for framing the corner squares. From the terracotta stripe cut eight strips 12½ × 4½ in/31.8 × 11.5 cm. From the burgundy fabric cut eight strips 1 in/2.5 cm wide across the full width of the fabric for the narrow border. Cut eight strips 3½ in/9 cm wide across the full width of the soft red fabric for the binding.

4. For the small appliqué blocks in the patchwork frame, cut 25 squares in assorted fabrics each 4½ × 4½ in/11.5 × 11.5 cm. This includes four center panel corners.

5. For the appliqué squares in the corner four-patches, cut eight 5 × 5 in/12.7 × 12.7 cm, all from the same fabric, if possible.

6. Cut the pieces for the appliqué motifs. The figures in our example were worked using needle-turning and blindhemming while the simple motifs were prepared with starch over pressing templates, and sewn with running stitch to provide visual variety.

7. Prepare the centers of flowers and stars by gathering over a template, as instructed in the General Techniques chapter.

SEWING

1. To make the background blocks, using a ¼ in/0.6 cm seam allowance, sew strips of the four shades of dyed calico plus the original undyed calico in a variety of sequences. There must be five strips in each set. Press then cross-cut into strips 4½ in/11.5 cm wide.

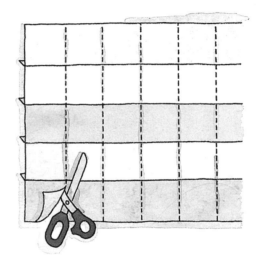

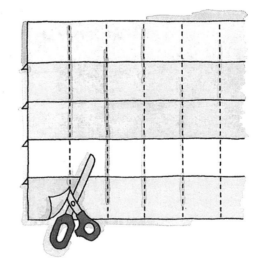

Seam together strips from the various combinations to make up the block units required, taking care when joining the strips to keep the top edge of each strip level. Make one unit of six strips for the Goosegirl; six units of five strips for the Blacksmith's Boy, Ploughman, Chickengirl, Milkmaid, Apple Picker, Shepherd; five units of four strips for the Swineherd, wreath, Churning Couple, Dancing Couple, Cowboy.

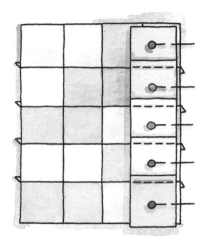

Label the blocks as you go. Put aside some leftover strips which will be used for assembling the borders together with the center.

2. Work all the twelve border appliqué blocks: the border blocks will not necessarily finish at the bottom of the fifth row of strips but are likely to be trimmed, so position the figures accordingly. Appliqué the setting strips with hearts, the corner blocks, the hourglass frame and the corner four-patch blocks.

3. Fold the center panel and fingerpress to give light guidelines for positioning the two figures. Slipstitch the figures in place and mark the panel to measure 25½ × 25½ in/65 × 65 cm. Do not trim at this point.

4. Using a ¼ in/0.6 cm seam allowance sew together a strip of geranium pink and a strip of purple. Repeat to make four sets. Press, then find the midpoint. With RS together and with the long raw edge of the strip against the marked line, pin to the center lines on two opposite sides of the center panel. Stitch, and press.

Repeat to attach the remaining two strips, then press carefully.

5. Select the four corner appliqués for the center panel and frame them with the extra strips of geranium pink on two sides. Check carefully which way they will fit in the quilt before sewing, so that the strips face inwards.

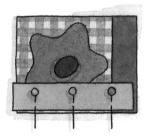

Press under ¼ in/0.6 cm turning on two sides, then lay the corner squares in position over the corners of the center panel, overlapping the ends of the framing strips and ensuring the corners are square. Appliqué the corner squares in place using the needle-turning technique and trim any excess background.

6. Make 85 hourglass blocks. To work two hourglass blocks at a time, mark a 5¼ in/13.4 cm square with one diagonal on the WS of a piece of fabric. Place this RS together with a second fabric and sew ¼ in/0.6 cm away from both sides of the diagonal. Cut along all drawn lines through both layers and press, usually towards the darker fabric. Mark the missing diagonal on the WS of one of the units.

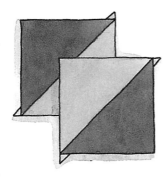

Place the two units RS together with the colors opposite. Sew both sides of the marked diagonals.

Cut between the lines of machine stitching to give two hourglass blocks. Press carefully.

To obtain units with four different colors, work two different pairings of fabric then combine one from each set at the next stage. It is best to mark the lighter fabric. Squares can be drawn adjacent to one another when the diagonals should be in opposite directions in neighboring squares to allow continuous sewing. To create the appearance of a scrap folk art quilt, do not make more than three squares-worth of the same fabric combination.

7. Mark squares 5¾ × 5¾ in/ 14.7 × 14.7 cm and work four units of the terracotta stripe fabric for the

corner four-patch blocks to the first cutting stage only. To make the stripes run in opposite directions in the finished units, place the fabrics RS together with the stripes parallel. Then pair each unit with a non-pieced square of exactly matching size with a third fabric, and proceed as before.

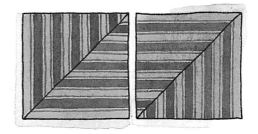

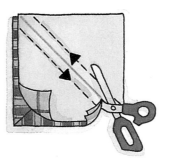

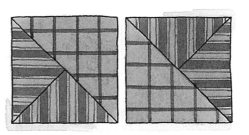

Arrange these blocks with the appliqué squares into four-patch units and assemble to make four corner blocks. Each block should measure 9½ in/24.2 cm square.

8. Following the illustration, lay out the hourglass blocks with the appliqué blocks. Place the setting strips with hearts between. Sew the blocks into rows and then assemble, pressing as you go. Attach one heart setting strip to both ends of the side units then join these to the sides of the center. Next join together a corner 9-block unit, a heart strip, the top unit, a second heart strip and a second corner unit. Repeat for the bottom row, then attach both these units to the center panel.

9. Each border unit is assembled slightly differently. Using the photograph as a guide, position each character in its right place. Begin with the Ploughman, wreath and Churning Couple. Sew these blocks together and join to the bottom edge of the center panel. Then join the Chickengirl, the Milkmaid and Dancing Couple. Add a corner four-patch beside the Chickengirl. From the spare pieced background strips add strips following the sequence in the diagram, noticing that the seams will not coincide because the units are of different sizes. Sew to the first border, then sew to the side of the quilt. Sew a four-patch to the Apple Picker and sew on border three. Attach a four-patch to each end of border four, then sew to the quilt. Press carefully.

The three illustrations below will help you follow the directions in step 7 to make the hourglass frame.

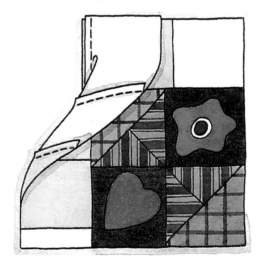

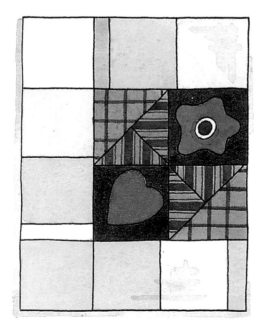

10. Sew the narrow burgundy strips in pairs with a ¼ in/0.6 cm straight seam pressed open.

11. Mark up the finished sides of the quilt but do not trim. Sew a narrow burgundy strip to the sides of the quilt, then to the top and bottom. Press and trim the excess block background fabric.

12. Spread out the backing, RS down, then the wadding and the quilt top, RS up. Pin and tack the layers together then quilt in-the-ditch around the central figures. Machine quilt the setting, the hourglass frame and the corner four-patch blocks. Behind the border figures quilt a landscape based on the the lower panels of the Shepherd and Swineherd quilts. Quilt the inside of the wreath with your name and date of completion.

13. After completing the quilting, trim the sides of the wadding and backing to 1¼ in/3.2 cm beyond the edge of the burgundy.

14. To finish the quilt, join the red binding strips into one length and press in half lengthwise. Sew the binding to the burgundy strip with ¼ in/0.6 cm seam allowance, following the directions for continuous binding in the General Techniques chapter on page 111. Take care to miter the fabric accurately at the corners because the binding is quite wide. Carefully fold the binding to the back of the quilt, and slipstitch securely in place to the stitching line.

General Techniques

While some knowledge of quiltmaking is assumed, this general techniques chapter is designed to fill in gaps for intermediate quilters and to introduce all the necessary basic skills to those new to the arts of appliqué, patchwork and quilting.

FABRIC CHOICE AND COLOR

The special character and charm of the "Sweet and Simple" quilts in this collection are largely due to the combination of fabrics chosen. Antique quilts made in the style we have come to know as "Folk Art" were worked in homespun fabrics, particularly the plaids and stripes of everyday working clothes and in the colors most easily achieved by home-dyeing. While superficially a simple group of fabrics, it is the variety of scale and complexity of design that offer an abundance of interest for the eye, plus the ability to create visual texture which is so useful for the kinds of pictorial designs featured in these projects.

To re-create the mood, collect as many directional fabrics – plaids and stripes – as you can. Try to include both small and large scale designs. Also, in addition to eye-catching patterns with plenty of contrast, look for patterns where the colors are very similar making the design subtle. Use recycled fabrics, but select only the least worn parts. Successful "Folk Art"

quilts owe a lot to never having enough of any one fabric. So one fabric never appears over-used or dominant. The need to substitute a scrap of similar color but different pattern, for example, can greatly enhance the finished project.

With quilts of this style, remember that you do not have to copy the exact color scheme illustrated. When changing the palette of large parts of the design, make up a reference card or a paper version of the plan with your substitutions clearly marked.

DYEING

Home-dyed fabrics, whether you use tea or commercial dye, can help to achieve the homespun look in these projects. Tea will bring an instant "aged" quality to a new piece of work, re-creating the appearance of an antique quilt. However, it can be difficult to repeat a particular shade and it is also prone to fading. Dylon has devised a cold water dye called Koala Brown to simulate tea-dyeing. It was used to prepare the four shades for the border of the Marriage Quilt.

Over-dyeing, by submerging printed fabrics in a dye bath, can add an antique look to otherwise modern material. This method will also unify a group of fabrics which are not to your color taste or needs. Remember that existing designs will absorb the dye in different and unpredictable ways giving you greater variety.

Before starting, thoroughly familiarize yourself with these instructions and those supplied with the dye product. Always wash and rinse new fabric before you begin to remove dressing and allow it to dry partially before submerging into the dye bath. As a precaution wear old clothes and rubber gloves. A plastic bucket or stainless steel basin is a suitable container for dyeing and use a piece of garden cane for stirring.

Materials: 1 tin of Koala Brown dye, 16 oz / 500 gm salt and 4 sachets of Dylon Cold Fix and up to 2 lb / 1 kg cotton fabric (dry weight).

Following the detailed instructions for mixing and using the dye, make up the solution using 1 pt / 500 ml of very hot water. From this, measure out decreasing quantities to obtain four successively lighter shades. Use a separate container for each dilution. Each solution will dye up to 8 oz/250 gm of cotton fabric.

To prepare the first dye bath for the darkest shade, put enough cold water in the container to allow the fabric to move about easily. Dissolve 4 oz/125 gm salt and 1 sachet Cold Fix in very hot water and add 8 fl oz/200 ml of the dye solution to the container. Stir well, then add the clean, damp fabric. Stir well for 15 minutes, then from time to time for the next 45 minutes. Take out the fabric, rinse to remove loose dye, then wash in hot water and dry.

Once you have got the first dye bath past the first 15 minutes, you can start the next dilution if sufficient containers are available. Repeat the above process for each tone, using the same amount of salt and Cold Fix each time but for a medium shade, 4 fl oz/100 ml of dye solution, for a light shade 2 fl oz/50 ml, for a pale shade 1 fl oz/25 ml.

After dyeing and rinsing each piece of fabric, the four shades can be safely washed together in the washing machine.

PATTERNS AND TEMPLATES

Full-size patterns have been supplied wherever possible. However, due to size constraints, we have needed to scale many patterns down. The easiest way to make a full-size pattern is to enlarge the appropriate amount on a photocopier. Alternatively, draw a grid of squares over the pattern and on an appropriately large sheet of paper draw a second grid of the correct size squares. Then, transfer the design, square by square onto the full-size grid. Several motifs and characters appear in more than one project in different sizes. In these cases, you will need to re-size the patterns as instructed to suit the required use.

Once the pattern is the correct size, a template must be made around which you can trace the design onto the fabric. Appliqué templates do not include seam allowances. Trace around the template on the right side (RS) of the fabric with a sharp, hard pencil or soap sliver, and add a scant ¼ in/0.6 cm turning allowance by eye as you cut out.

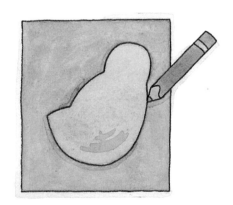

If you only need to cut one appliqué motif, tape the pattern over a light box (or on a window to use the daylight) then simply lay the fabric over, right side up, and trace around the appropriate shape. Cut out the shape, adding the turning by eye.

Template-free cutting instructions are given for pieced blocks using a quilters' rule and rotary cutter. Strip cutting may also be done by ruling out the required grid with a pencil and then cutting with scissors.

If you prefer the traditional method using templates, first decide whether you will piece the block design by hand or machine. Templates for hand-piecing are usually made without seam allowances and those for machine-piecing must include seam allowances. Templates for blocks can be made by tracing the drafted block design carefully onto typing paper. Cut this apart neatly and stick one of each shape onto card or sandpaper. More durable templates which will be used many times for large projects are best made from clear template plastic which can be laid directly over the original for marking. It is best not to make templates from photocopies for pieced blocks. Having cut the templates, it is wise to work a sample block before cutting up yardage for the whole project.

Label templates and identify the right side. If plastic seems difficult to mark, a small piece of masking tape can be stuck on the right side (RS) for writing on.

CUTTING

Fabric requirements are based on an economical use of materials, but do include an allowance for the occasional error. As a general rule, the largest pieces are listed for cutting first, leaving the smaller pieces to be cut from the remaining yardage. Before trimming border or sashing strips, always check the actual size you require by measuring the block or quilt body across its center, not at the edges. Mark this measurement along the sashing or border strip before easing on as necessary. Do not cut off any excess until stitching is completed.

Wherever the method is suitable, measurements are given for template-free cutting. For example, to cut a quantity of squares, begin by cutting strips of the size required and then cross-cut these to provide the necessary number of squares. For this method, the sizes quoted always include seam allowances.

When this strip-cutting method is not suitable, place templates for hand-piecing on the wrong side (WS) of the fabric or on the right side (RS) for appliqué. Trace around the template using a hard, sharp pencil. The pencil line is your stitching line. Cut the shape out carefully, including the seam allowance by eye.

HAND-PIECING

Lay the patches right side (RS) together, matching the ends of the seams and sew along the pencil line with a running stitch. At the end, take a backstitch. Do not sew across the seam allowance.

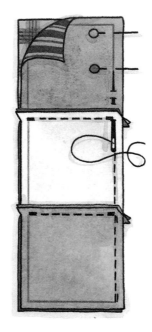

MACHINE-PIECING

Match the cut edges of the pieces and take care to sew a straight and accurate ¼ in/0.6 cm seam. If you use the edge of the presser foot as a guide: measure the seam allowance made with the same instrument used for cutting the pieces. As a rule, always use the same measuring tool throughout a project.

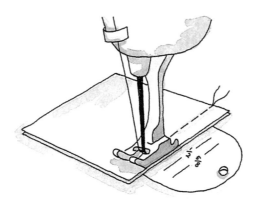

If your presser foot does not measure ¼ in/0.6 cm, adjust the sewing position of the needle or mark a guide line on the throat plate of the machine with a strip of masking tape.

Seams are stitched from one edge across to the other. Pairs of pieces can be chained one after another, but always make a stitch or two of thread between each pair so that they do not come undone when snipped apart later. Match corners and edges precisely.

When joining elements of a block or rows of squares, the appearance is improved by matching internal seams carefully even if the outer edges are not exactly aligned. However, if you are aiming for the random, haphazard look often associated with folk art quilts, then your seams need not always match perfectly! Try to be judicious about which seams matter.

APPLIQUÉ

All the projects in this book feature appliqué and several different approaches can be followed. In each project, the directions indicate which method was used for the example illustrated so that you can achieve similar results, even though any of the appliqué methods may be used. However, if you choose to use bonding when it was not the original method used, you will need to add an appropriate amount of fusible web to the Materials list.

Preparation for traditional (non-bonded) appliqué
The secret of good appliqué is thought by many to lie in good preparation. Try some of the following suggestions to see which works best for you.

Fingerpressing: Pinch a fold along the pencil line of each shape, before stitching. Take care not to stretch the edges as you pinch.

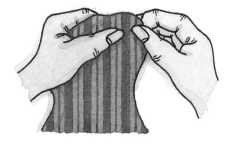

You will need to clip the inside curves as you approach them during stitching. Don't expect the turning to stay under. The fabric will "remember" where the fold was when you "stroke" it under with the tip of your needle.

Tacking: Fingerpress and fold under the turning in the same careful manner then tack it in place. This is particularly helpful when working complicated designs where all the parts must fit together accurately. This method allows you to see exactly where the finished edge of the shape will be. An example might be on a figure where the head and feet need to be attached before the garment. Tacking the turning on the garment helps to correctly position the head and feet. You can choose to do this just on some pieces of the design. For simpler components you can combine tacking with other preparation methods as appropriate.

Pressing templates and starch: When working several of the same simple shapes, make a pressing template from stiff cardboard. This should not be so thick as to make a ridge around the shape but firm enough not to buckle from the heat of an iron. Use the template to draw the motif on the wrong side (WS) of the fabric, then cut out. After clipping any inside curves, replace the template over the marked

shape. Spray some starch into a small container and with a paintbrush or cotton bud, paint starch onto the turning of the shape. The fabric needs to be quite saturated before pressing it firmly over the edge of the template with just the point of the iron.

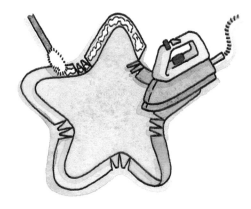

When dry and cold, ease out the template and repeat the process with the next piece.

Freezer paper: There are many different ways of using freezer paper in appliqué, but in all cases begin with the finished size template, without turnings. To make perfect circles, for example, iron the waxy side of the freezer paper to the wrong side (WS) of the fabric, then run a gathering thread through the seam allowance all around the shape.

Draw up to fit the template, secure but do not cut the thread. Spray with a puff of starch on the back to help press the turning.

Ease out the freezer paper before sewing in place using the thread already attached. The template can be used several times before it loses its waxiness.

For other shapes, iron the freezer paper to the wrong side (WS) and use the crispness of its edge inside the fabric to guide where you turn under the seam allowance. You can fingerpress first, or simply turn the seam allowance under as you stitch. Ease out the template with a needle before sewing the last bit, or cut away the background fabric to free the paper.

Alternatively, place the freezer paper with shiny side up, on the wrong side (WS) of the fabric, then use just the point of the iron to press the seam allowance onto the waxy surface to hold it in place.

Preparation for bonded appliqué

To prepare the appliqué pieces, use a paper-backed fusible web or adhesive powder following the manufacturer's instructions.

Trace each design element onto the paper side of the web, reversing them as required. Cut out allowing a small margin all around. Using an iron set on "wool," fuse the webbing (rough side down) to the wrong side (WS) of the appliqué fabric. When cold, cut out the appliqué shape on the pencil line.

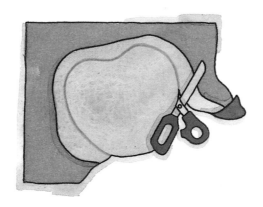

Peel away the paper backing then position correctly on the background and fuse again. Do not handle until cold.

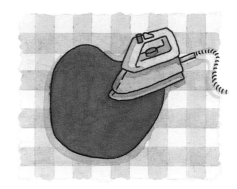

SEWING

Hand appliqué

A demonstration of good sewing skill is to be able to appliqué as invisibly as possible. Consequently one of the most popular appliqué stitches is the blindhem stitch.

The running stitch, used for both hand-piecing and quilting, can also be used for stitching the appliqué shape to the background, though this tends to be much more visible. It can also add both a slight texture to the work and visual variety through the choice of thread color.

Even more opportunity for texture and color variation derives from the use of blanket or buttonhole stitch to secure appliqué shapes.

Machine appliqué
To simulate a hand-sewn blindhem stitch, prepare the turnings on the shape to be stitched, then sew using the blindhem stitch on your sewing machine. This works best if a good color match exists between fabric and thread. Clear or smoke monofilament, as used for quilting, is both effective and difficult to see! Take care when pressing these nylon threads as some are more sensitive to heat than others.

To cover the raw edges of bonded appliqué pieces, use blanket stitch or whipped chain stitch by hand, or machine satin stitch.

Set your machine for a very short stitch length and a medium width zigzag stitch, and match your thread color to the appliqué pieces rather than to the background color. Test your stitch tension on a scrap first. You may need to loosen the top tension a little to pull the thread to the wrong side. The stitches should form a solid band of color about ⅛ in/0.3 cm wide. For items that will not receive heavy wear, stitching is not essential.

PRESSING

Generally press patchwork seams to one side, usually towards the darker fabric. Always press seams before sewing the next unit across them. Where possible press seams on adjoining rows in opposite directions so that they interlock when matched.

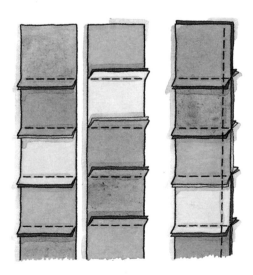

To avoid flattening appliqué during pressing put a thick, fluffy hand towel on the ironing board, then lay the appliqué face down over it and

press from the back. If you find the texture of your towel can be seen on the front of the work, just place a clean tea towel or pressing cloth over it before putting on the appliqué block.

After trimming away loose ends and threads from the back of the completed quilt top, always give a final press before assembling the three quilt layers.

THE QUILTING DESIGN

With each project, suggestions are given for suitable and typical quilting designs. You may like to substitute your own ideas, but try to keep the rustic style.

Many designs do not have to be marked onto the quilt top before putting the layers together. These include:

1. In-the-ditch – quilting along the seam lines of pieced blocks or immediately next to appliqué motifs.

2. Echo or outline quilt – quilting approximately ¼ in/0.6 cm away from seam lines, marking a line at a time with ¼ in/0.6 cm masking tape or working by eye.

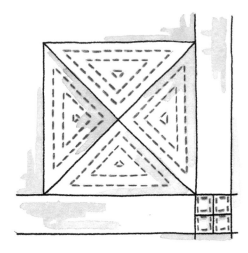

3. Simple filling grids also marked by masking tape.

4. Templates cut from adhesive-backed plastic can be bought ready-made from quilting shops, or the plastic is available in sheets. Trace your chosen motifs and cut out carefully. Peel off the backing, position the first template on the quilt top and press down firmly. Quilt around the motif, moving it along as necessary. Each template can be re-used several times before the adhesive is exhausted. You will need several copies of motifs that appear repeatedly.

5. Square knot tying or tufting: using thicker yarn such as crochet cotton, take two overlapping stitches through all layers and tie off with a double knot.

Other designs need to be marked on the whole quilt top before the layers are assembled. Put the quilt top on a firm surface and tape down the corners. Draw around the chosen quilting templates with a sharp pencil. Dark fabrics can be marked with a light-colored pencil, or a sharpened sliver of soap.

ASSEMBLING THE QUILT LAYERS

Press the backing fabric and spread out right side (RS) down on a flat surface. Secure the edges with masking tape (to floor or table) or with pins (to carpet). Center the wadding on top, smoothing out any wrinkles without stretching it. Center the prepared quilt top, right side up, on the wadding. If you need to re-position the quilt top, do not drag it over the wadding. Lift it carefully to avoid crumpling the

wadding. Pin the layers together and baste thoroughly from the center outwards every 4 in/10.2 cm. For hand-quilting in a hoop or on the lap, the basting needs to be closer than if the quilt is to be fixed into a frame. If planning to machine-quilt, the layers can be pin-basted with fine, stainless steel safety pins, which will not stain or leave holes. Be warned that you will need one safety pin every 2 in/5.1 cm for adequate basting.

FINISHING

Three common ways to finish the edges of a quilt are used in the projects selected for this book.

Fold-finishing
After quilting, trim the top and backing to the required size plus ½ in/1.3 cm turnings. Trim the wadding to the finished quilt size. Fold both sets of turnings to the inside, with one of them wrapped over the edge of the wadding to enclose it, and so that both edges are even. Either machine sew through all layers, slipstitch the folded edges together, OR sew together with a running stitch to match the quilting.

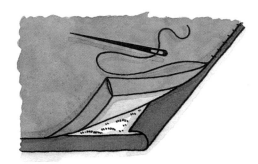

Self-binding

For this finishing technique, either the backing or the quilt top needs to be ¾ – 1 in/1.9 – 2.5 cm larger than the finished quilt. If you intend to bring the backing around to the front, choose backing fabric that complements the quilt top.

Trim the top and wadding to the finished size and trim the backing to include your turning allowance.

Fold the backing over to the front, turn in the raw edge, and pin or baste. Fold the corners into a neat miter. Machine topstitch or blindhem the edges to the front of the quilt by hand.

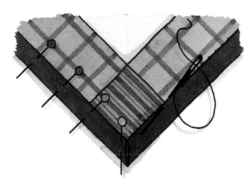

If you choose the latter, add one or two lines of quilting stitches all around the inside edge to secure the wadding.

To bring the quilt top around to the backing for self-binding, simply reverse the instructions.

Separate binding

This is a popular finishing technique because it gives a firm edge, wears well and offers a final opportunity to add a color statement to a quilt. Usually binding strips are cut twice the desired width, plus ½ in/1.3 cm for turnings, across the straight grain of the fabric. Only when the quilt has curved or scalloped edges does the binding have to be cut on the bias, unless the fabric design contributes something special when cut this way, as in the case of plaids.

Bindings can be single or double thickness. The following instructions are for single binding. Cut sufficient strips of fabric 1¼ in/3.2 cm wide to equal the perimeter of the quilt plus about 10 in/25.4 cm. Join the strips into a continuous length using diagonal seams: lay two strips right sides facing and ends even, then turn one at right angles to the other still with edges even. Sew diagonally across the double layer and press open.

Place the binding on the right side (RS) of the quilt with right sides (RS) together, beginning partway along one side and not at a corner.

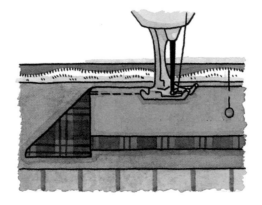

Fold in the beginning of the binding and continue to pin and stitch the binding in place until exactly ¼ in/0.6 cm from the corner. Backstitch a short distance, then remove the quilt from the machine. Fold the binding up at a 45 degree angle, then back down to align it with the adjacent edge of the quilt top, giving you the bulk to fold the binding to the back.

Make sure the folds are sharp and exactly in line with the edges of the quilt top.

Pin and stitch, repeating the process to turn the remaining corners neatly. At the end, allow enough binding to overlap the start, and trim away any excess. Continue stitching through the overlap to secure the binding where it meets.

Fold the binding to the back of the quilt, and hem in place along the stitching line.

Take special care at the corners when attaching extra wide separate binding. To achieve a perfectly square corner, make sure to fold the binding fully to the edges.

CONTINUOUS BIAS FOR BINDING

Exactly how much bias is obtained depends on how large a piece of fabric is used and how wide the binding needs to be. As a guide, a rectangle 9 × 36 in/22.8 × 91.4 cm will make about 7 yd/6.4 m of bias 1 in/2.5 cm wide or about 5¼ yd or just under 5 m of bias 1½ in/ 3.8 cm wide. The exact proportions of your piece of fabric do not matter as long as the rectangle is true to the grain and has nice square corners.

1. Iron the fabric and have it on a firm surface, right side (RS) down.

2. Find the true bias by folding one corner over so that the vertical side aligns with the bottom edge. Crease without stretching and cut along this line. Repeat at the opposite corner by folding it up so that the vertical aligns with the top edge. Again crease and cut. If short of fabric, instead of this last cut, the first triangle cut off may simply be moved to the other end of the rectangle and stitched on with a very narrow seam (pressed open).

3. In pencil mark out the width of binding required by measuring from the first diagonal at right angles the appropriate amount as many times as will fit in. It will be necessary to reposition the ruler but take care to keep it at right angles to the first edge. Connect up the marks made so that there will be continuous lines to cut along later. Do not worry if the fabric is not exactly divisible by the width of the strip you require.

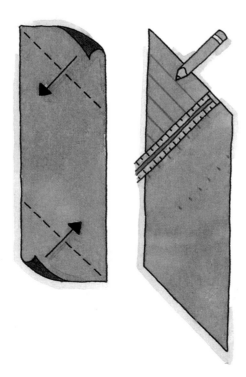

4. Along the top and bottom edges rule a line ¼ in/0.6 cm from the edge. These will be the sewing lines. Take note of points A and B on the diagram. A is right at the beginning of the fabric and B is on the opposite side where the first ruled line meets the sewing line.

5. Insert a pin at point A and, folding the fabric with right side (RS) inside, pass the pin through point B. If the fabric is held up to the light it should be possible to see a sort of cross formed by the matched lines where they meet at the sewing line. Continue to match each of the lines on the top edge with the corresponding line on the opposite edge. Do not worry that at first these edges do not seem to lie together naturally: they will form a spiralling seam around the fabric tube. There must be a "step" at the beginning of the sewing line.

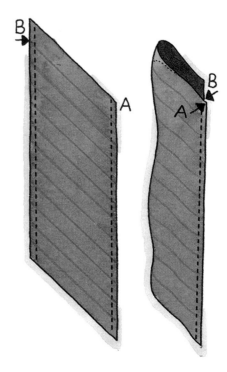

6. Now sew the seam along the marked sewing line using a short stitch length, say 20 stitches per 1 in/2.5 cm. After checking that none of the ruled lines have shifted, press the seam open.

7. Beginning at the matched A and B points start cutting round the spiral along the lines marked.

HANGING SLEEVES

Sleeves can be added to both quilts and small wallhangings if they are likely to be displayed at any time. A double sleeve is best as it reduces the risk of splinters entering the quilt from a batten. It requires a piece of fabric about 10 in/25.4 cm deep and approximately the width of the quilt. Large quilts often have a two-part sleeve, so that they can be supported at three points. They may also benefit from having a sleeve and batten attached to the lower edge as well. For small hanging, which may be hung on lightweight dowels, make a sleeve 5 in/12.7 cm deep.

1. Press and stitch a narrow hem on both short ends.

2. Fold in half with right sides (RS) out and sew the long edges together to make a tube. Press the seam open, in the center of the tube.

3. Place the sleeve with this seam towards the quilt backing and hand stitch in place, including the layer at the short ends so that the pole cannot be slipped into the wrong aperture.

SIGNING YOUR WORK

Always sign your work, at least with your name and the date of completion. Add an inscription or dedication if you wish. Labels can be embroidered by hand, cross stitched, machine embroidered or written with indelible fabric pens, then stitched neatly to the backing.

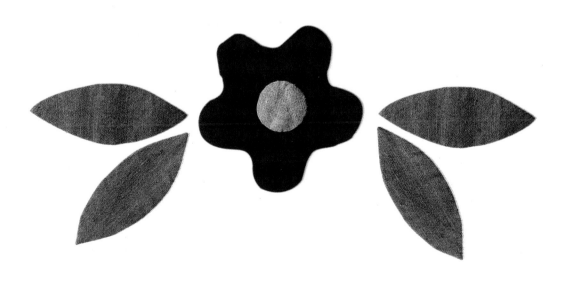

Templates

Cow: enlarge to 9 in / 22.8 cm for Marriage quilt

To produce templates of the correct size for your projects, draw a line between the two red markers. Enlarge or reduce on a photocopier to bring the line to the required length.

Milkmaid & cow: enlarge to 12⅜ in / 31.4 cm for Homestead quilt

Flower: enlarge to 5¾ in / 14.6 cm for Homestead quilt

Homestead: enlarge to 15 in / 38.1 cm for Homestead quilt

Jug: enlarge to 3¾ in/9.5 cm for Homestead quilt

Churning couple: enlarge to 17 in/43.2 cm for Homestead quilt

enlarge to 11¾ in/29.8 cm for Marriage quilt

Oak leaf: enlarge to 7⅝ in/19.4 cm for Homestead quilt

reduce to 1½ in/3.8 cm for Tote bag

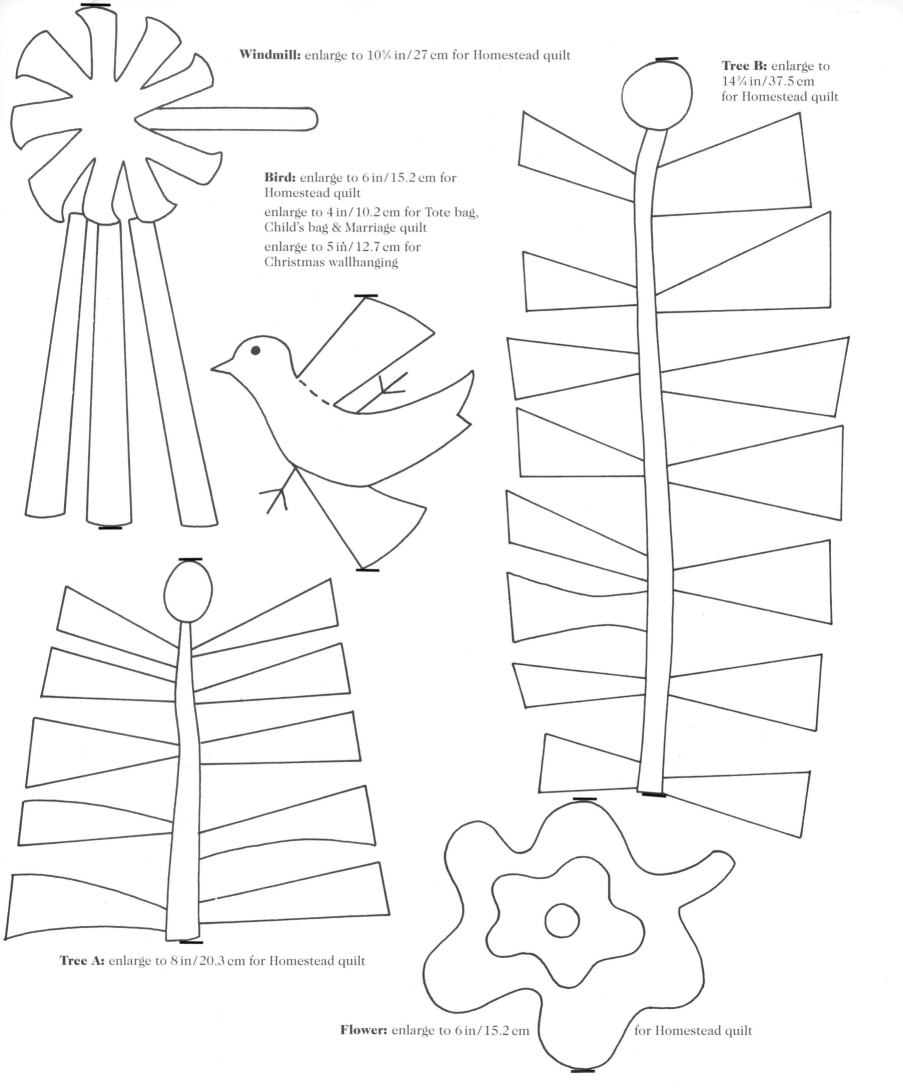

Windmill: enlarge to 10⅝ in/27 cm for Homestead quilt

Tree B: enlarge to 14¾ in/37.5 cm for Homestead quilt

Bird: enlarge to 6 in/15.2 cm for Homestead quilt

enlarge to 4 in/10.2 cm for Tote bag, Child's bag & Marriage quilt

enlarge to 5 in/12.7 cm for Christmas wallhanging

Tree A: enlarge to 8 in/20.3 cm for Homestead quilt

Flower: enlarge to 6 in/15.2 cm for Homestead quilt

Tree C: enlarge to 12 in/30.5 cm for Homestead quilt

Nesting hen: enlarge to 7½ in/19 cm for Chickengirl quilt & Nesting hen cushion

Tab: same size for Tote bag and Child's bag

Fox: enlarge to 7 in/17.8 cm for Chickengirl quilt Same size for Farmyard playmat

117

Chickengirl: enlarge to 23 in/58.4 cm for Chickengirl quilt

enlarge to 9¼ in/23.5 cm for Marriage quilt

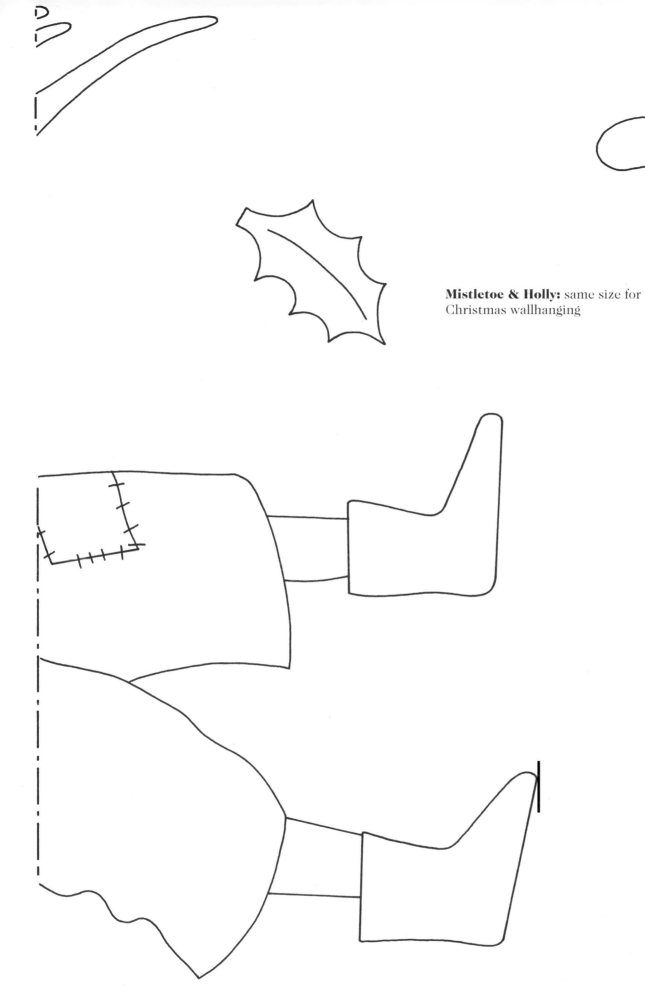

Mistletoe & Holly: same size for Christmas wallhanging

Sleeping fox: same size
for Chickengirl quilt
enlarge to 9 in/22.9 cm
for Sleeping fox cushion

Chick: same size for Chickengirl quilt,
Kitchen Chicks apron & Oven mitts

120

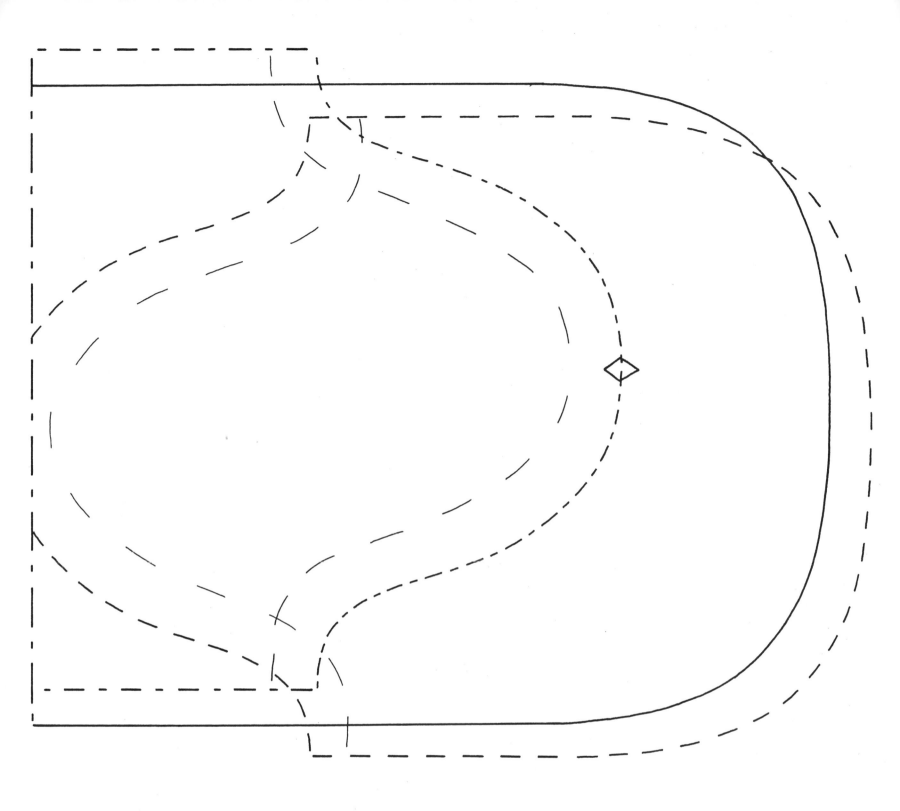

Oven Mitt pattern: same size

Oven Mitt Back A
Oven Mitt Upper Palm B
Oven Mitt Lower Palm C

Waist Tie placement

Join pattern here

Pocket Outline

Kitchen Chicks apron pattern: same size

Center front – place on fold of fabric

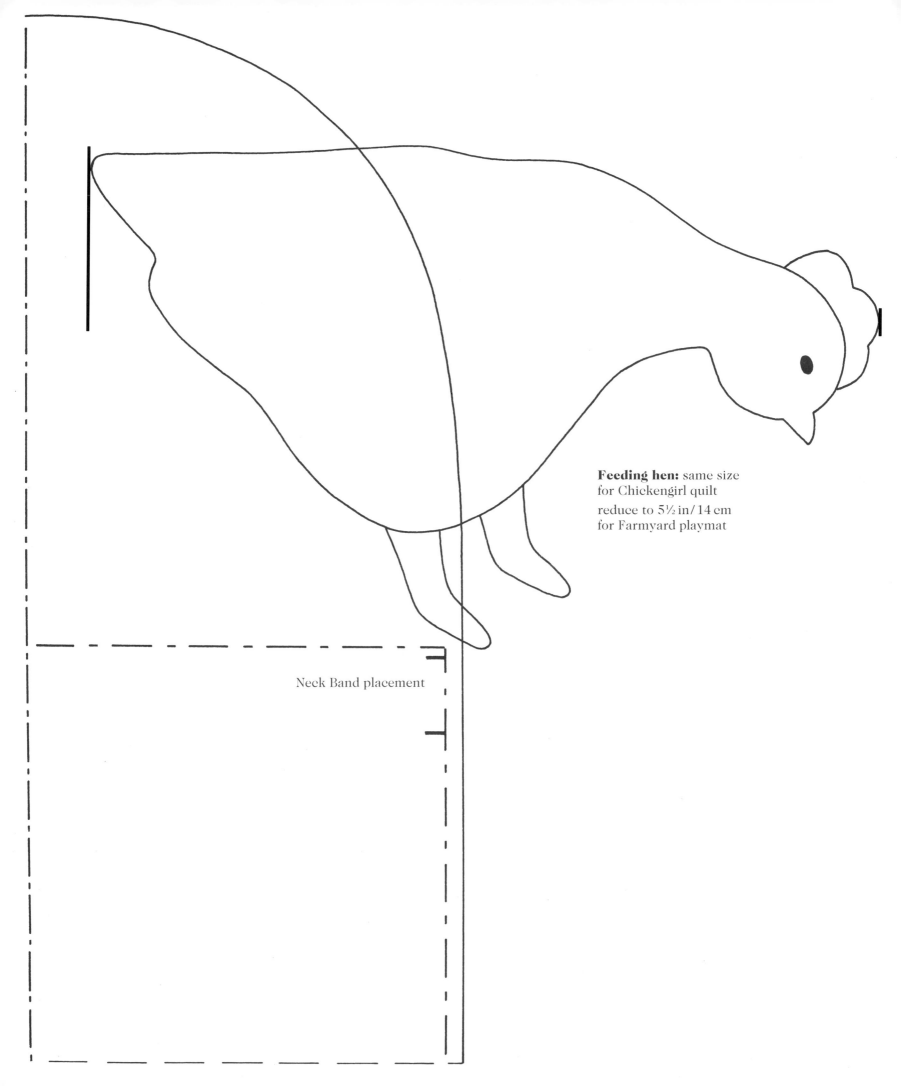

Feeding hen: same size
for Chickengirl quilt

reduce to 5½ in / 14 cm
for Farmyard playmat

Neck Band placement

Dancing Couples: enlarge to 10 in / 25.4 cm for Dancing Couple wallhanging & Marriage quilt

Dancing Couples silhouette: same size

Dancing dog: same size for Dancing Couples wallhanging

enlarge to 4½ in / 11.4 cm for Sampler wallhanging & Apple Picker quilt

enlarge to 11 in / 28 cm for cushion

All templates on this page are same size for Dancing Couples wallhanging

Cockerel:
enlarge to
4⅝ in/
11.7 cm for
Farmyard playmat

enlarge to 9¼ in/
23.5 cm for cushion

Add separate wing detail

Girl: same size for Apple Picker quilt
reduce to 9 in / 22.8 cm for Marriage quilt

Bird: same size for Apple Picker quilt and Picnic placemats

For bird in branches, cut out on broken line, then appliqué or embroider separate wing

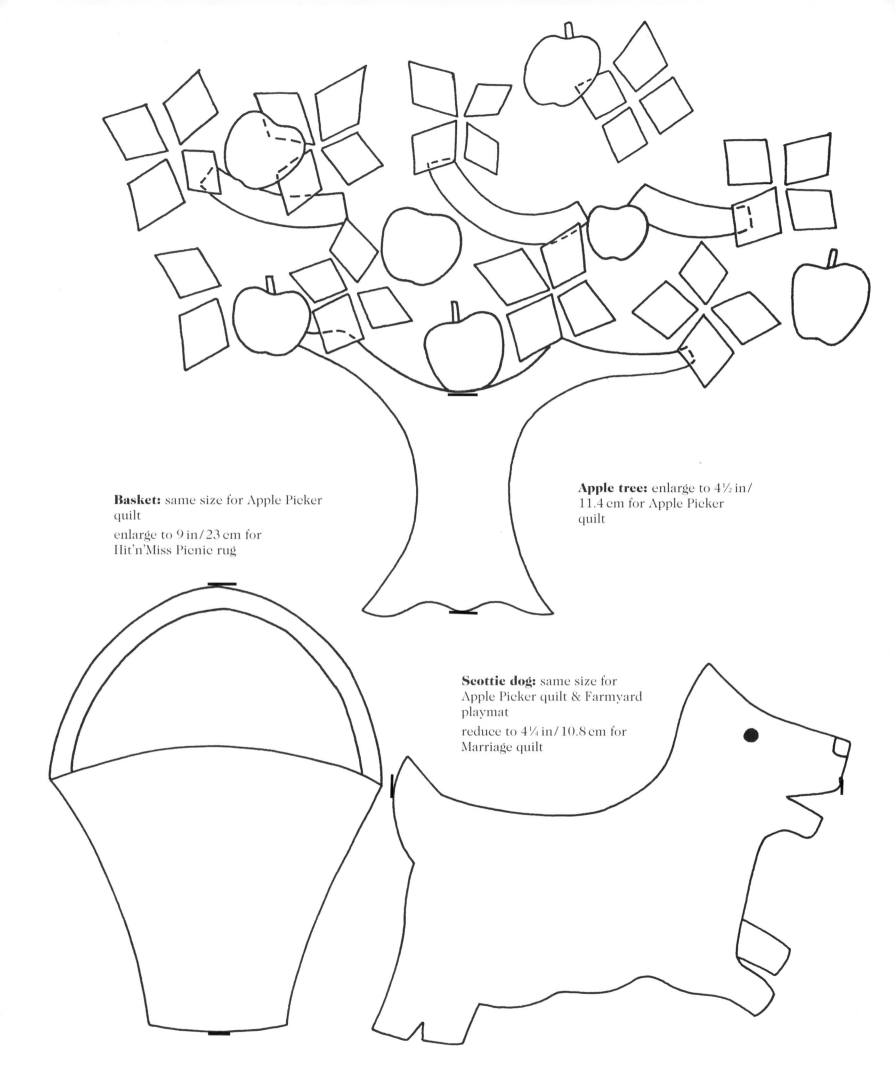

Basket: same size for Apple Picker quilt

enlarge to 9 in/23 cm for Hit'n'Miss Picnic rug

Apple tree: enlarge to 4½ in/ 11.4 cm for Apple Picker quilt

Scottie dog: same size for Apple Picker quilt & Farmyard playmat

reduce to 4¼ in/10.8 cm for Marriage quilt

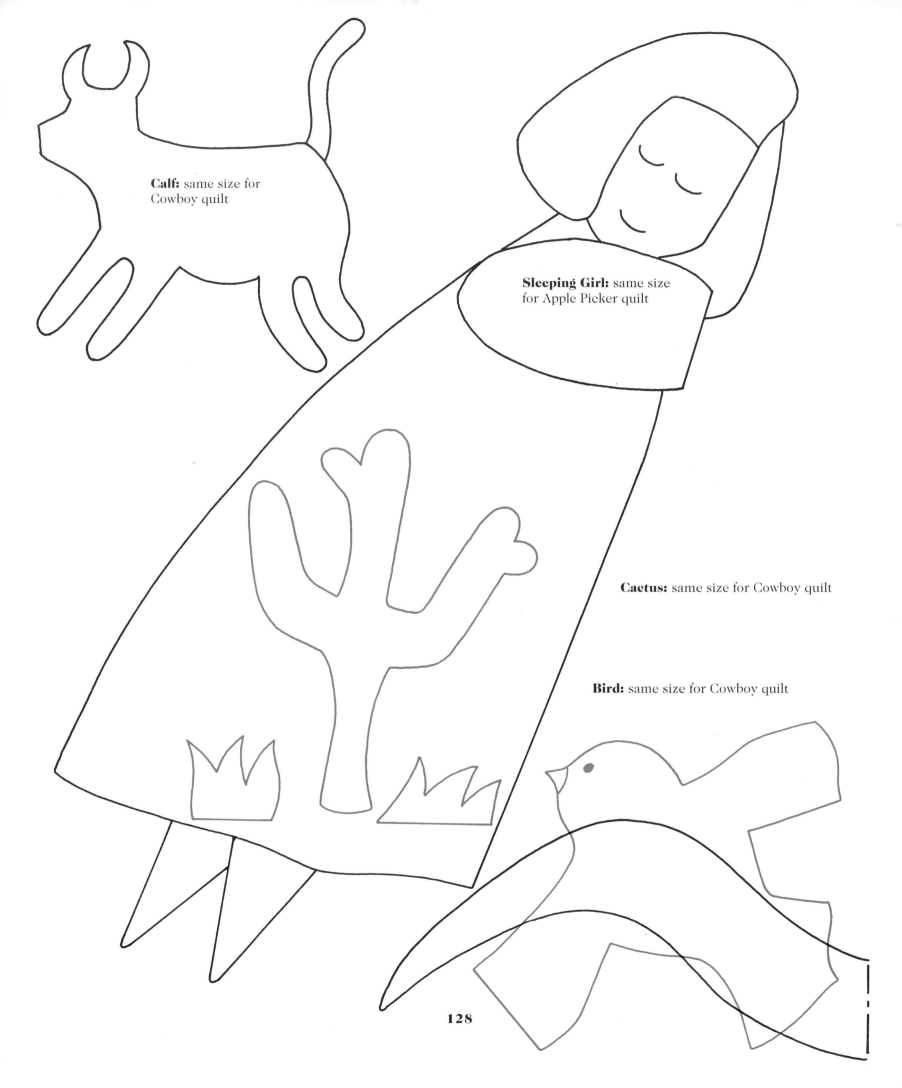

Calf: same size for Cowboy quilt

Sleeping Girl: same size for Apple Picker quilt

Cactus: same size for Cowboy quilt

Bird: same size for Cowboy quilt

128

Star:
same size for
Cowboy quilt

Cowboy: same size for Cowboy quilt
enlarge to 11 in/28 cm for Cowboy
cushion and Marriage quilt

Snake: same size for Cowboy quilt

129

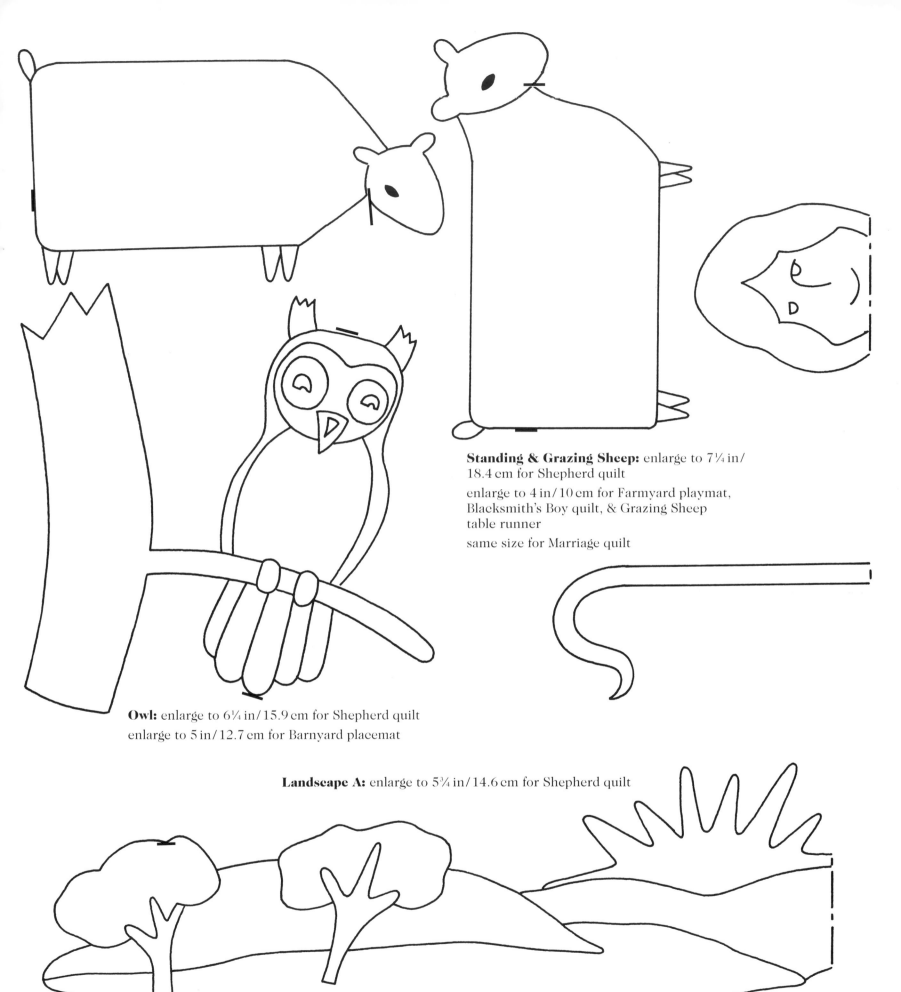

Standing & Grazing Sheep: enlarge to 7¼ in/ 18.4 cm for Shepherd quilt

enlarge to 4 in/ 10 cm for Farmyard playmat, Blacksmith's Boy quilt, & Grazing Sheep table runner

same size for Marriage quilt

Owl: enlarge to 6¼ in/ 15.9 cm for Shepherd quilt
enlarge to 5 in/ 12.7 cm for Barnyard placemat

Landscape A: enlarge to 5¾ in/ 14.6 cm for Shepherd quilt

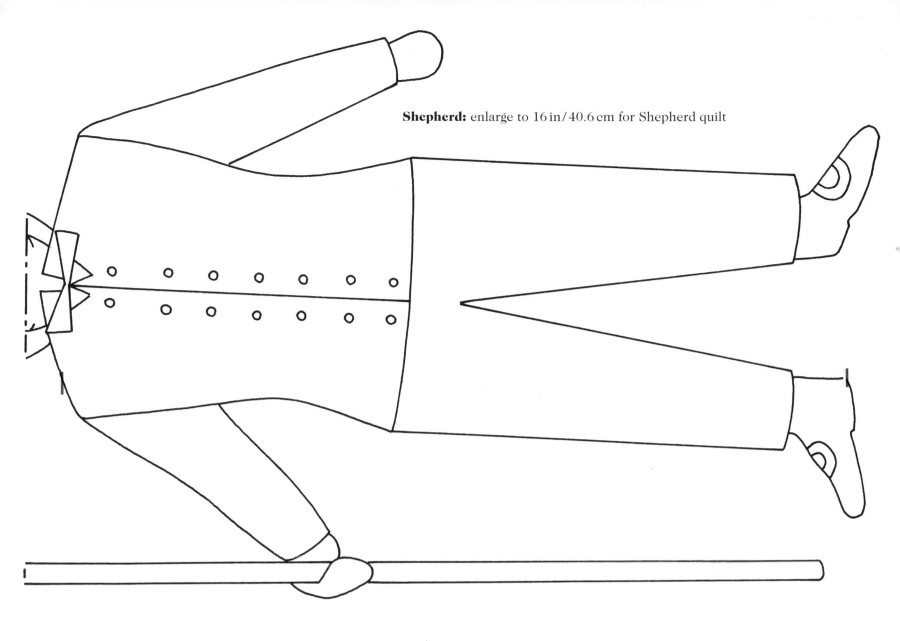

Shepherd: enlarge to 16 in/40.6 cm for Shepherd quilt

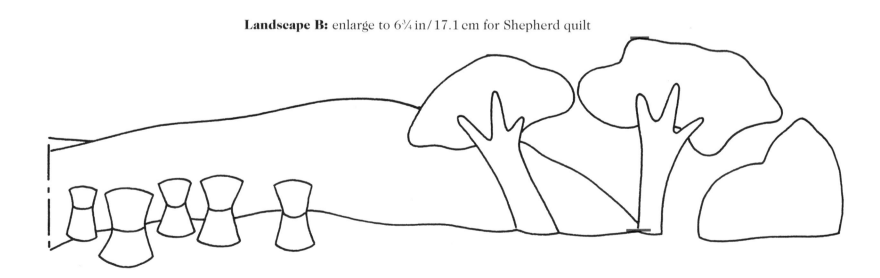

Landscape B: enlarge to 6¾ in/17.1 cm for Shepherd quilt

Goosegirl: enlarge to 20 in / 50.8 cm for Goosegirl wallhanging

enlarge to 11¼ in / 28.6 cm for Marriage quilt

Goose A: enlarge to 10½ in / 26.7 cm for Goose Chase tablecloth

enlarge to 3¾ in / 9.5 cm for Marriage quilt

Goose B: enlarge to 5 in / 12.7 cm for Farmyard playmat

enlarge to 4 in / 10.2 cm for Marriage quilt

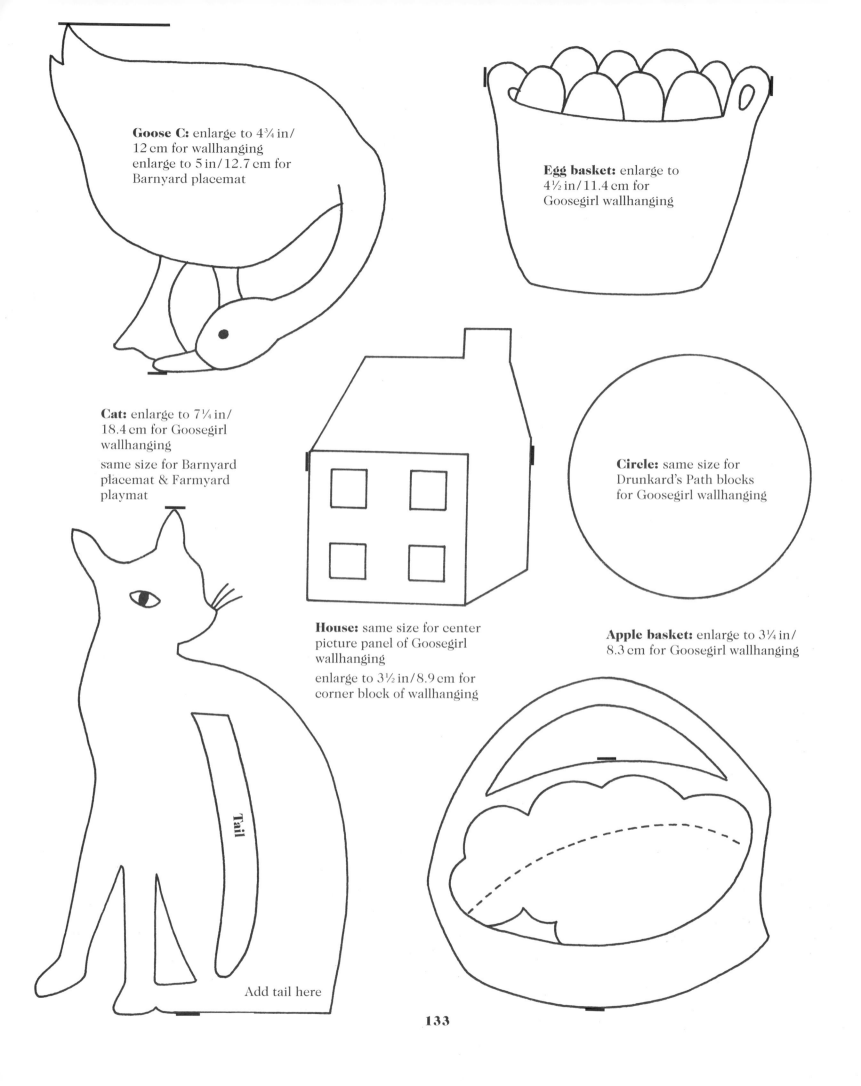

Goose C: enlarge to 4¾ in/ 12 cm for wallhanging enlarge to 5 in/12.7 cm for Barnyard placemat

Egg basket: enlarge to 4½ in/11.4 cm for Goosegirl wallhanging

Cat: enlarge to 7¼ in/ 18.4 cm for Goosegirl wallhanging

same size for Barnyard placemat & Farmyard playmat

Circle: same size for Drunkard's Path blocks for Goosegirl wallhanging

House: same size for center picture panel of Goosegirl wallhanging

enlarge to 3½ in/8.9 cm for corner block of wallhanging

Apple basket: enlarge to 3¼ in/ 8.3 cm for Goosegirl wallhanging

Tail

Add tail here

133

Wreath: ¼ pattern only. Same size for Goose Chase tablecloth & Marriage quilt

Dog: same size for Blacksmith's Boy quilt

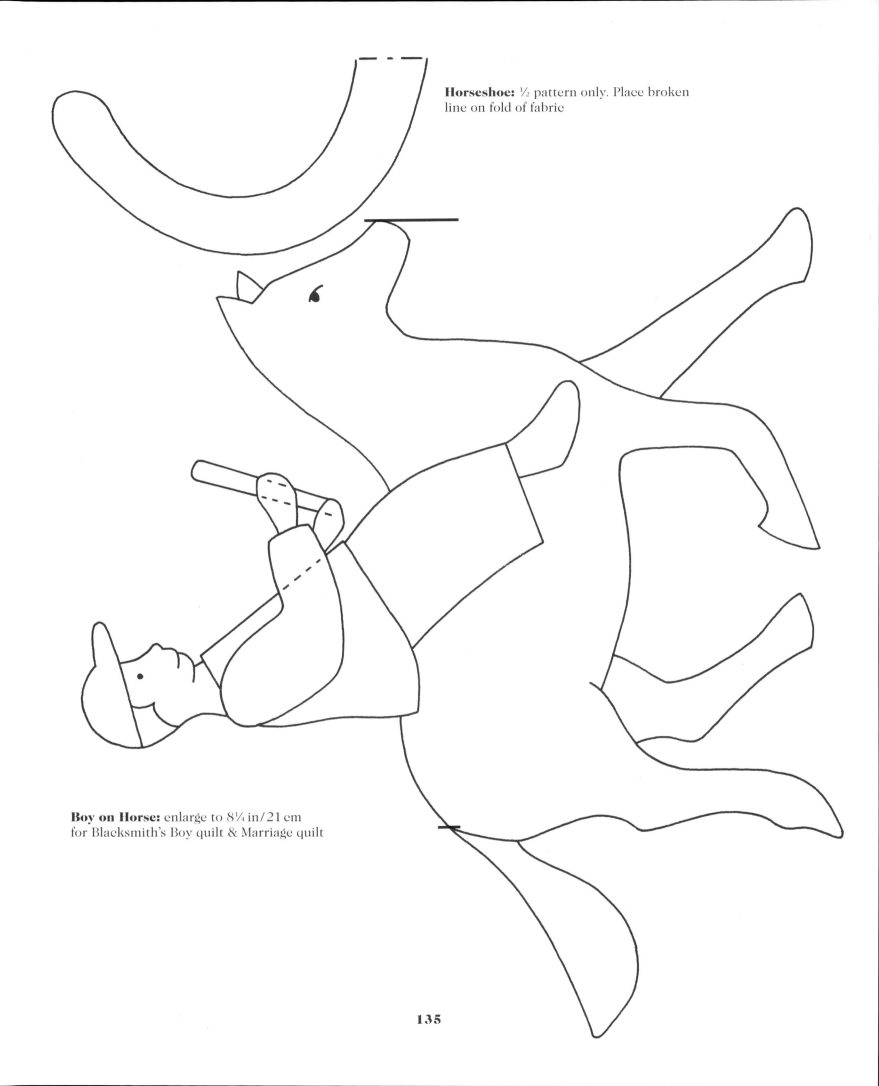

Horseshoe: ½ pattern only. Place broken line on fold of fabric

Boy on Horse: enlarge to 8¼ in/21 cm for Blacksmith's Boy quilt & Marriage quilt

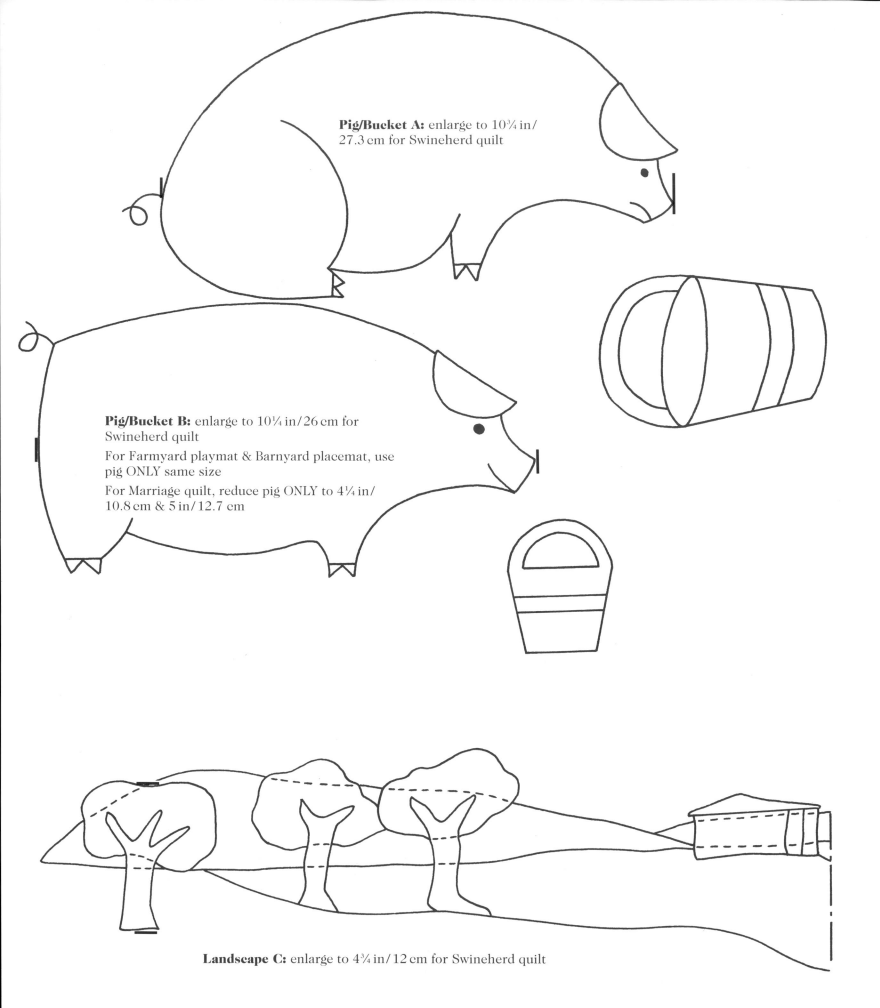

Pig/Bucket A: enlarge to 10¾ in/
27.3 cm for Swineherd quilt

Pig/Bucket B: enlarge to 10¼ in/26 cm for
Swineherd quilt

For Farmyard playmat & Barnyard placemat, use
pig ONLY same size

For Marriage quilt, reduce pig ONLY to 4¼ in/
10.8 cm & 5 in/12.7 cm

Landscape C: enlarge to 4¾ in/12 cm for Swineherd quilt

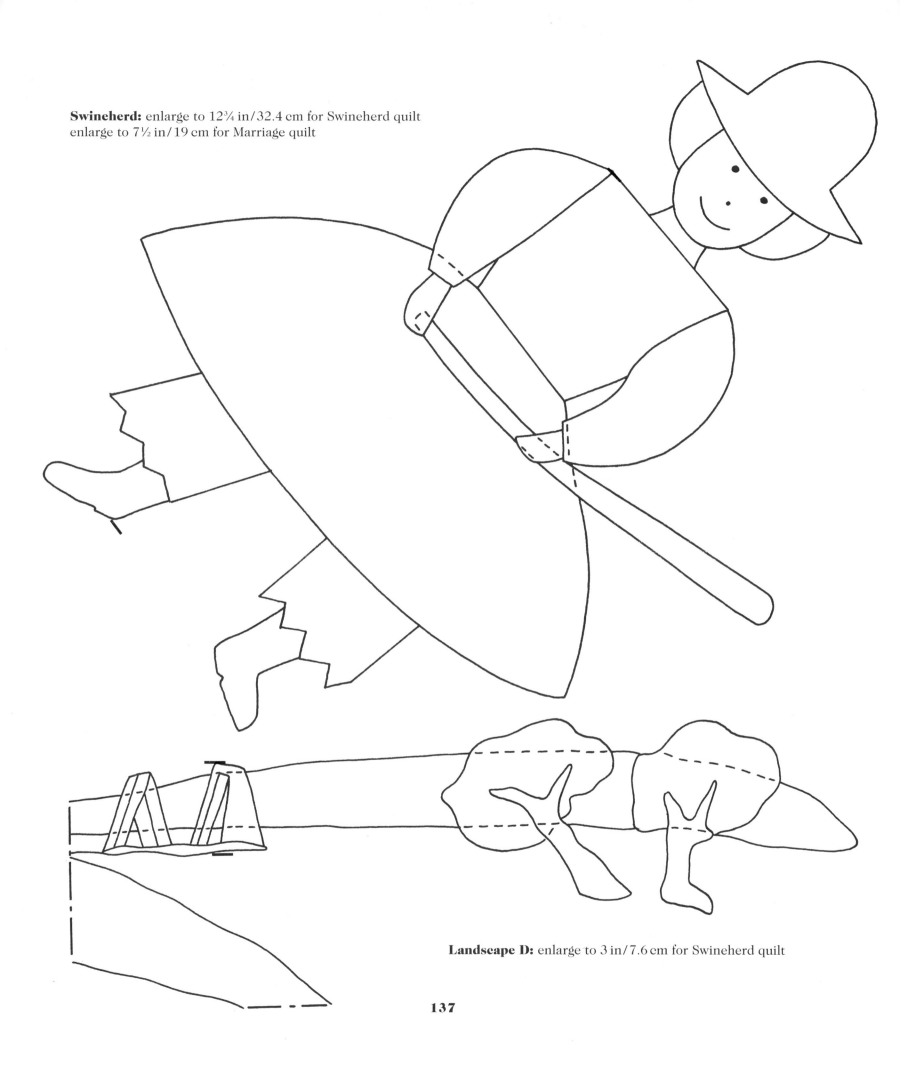

Swineherd: enlarge to 12¾ in/32.4 cm for Swineherd quilt
enlarge to 7½ in/19 cm for Marriage quilt

Landscape D: enlarge to 3 in/7.6 cm for Swineherd quilt

Wedding Couple: enlarge to 17 in/43.2 cm for Marriage quilt

Ploughman/horse: all templates same size for Ploughman wallhanging

enlarge to 7 in / 17.8 cm for Marriage quilt

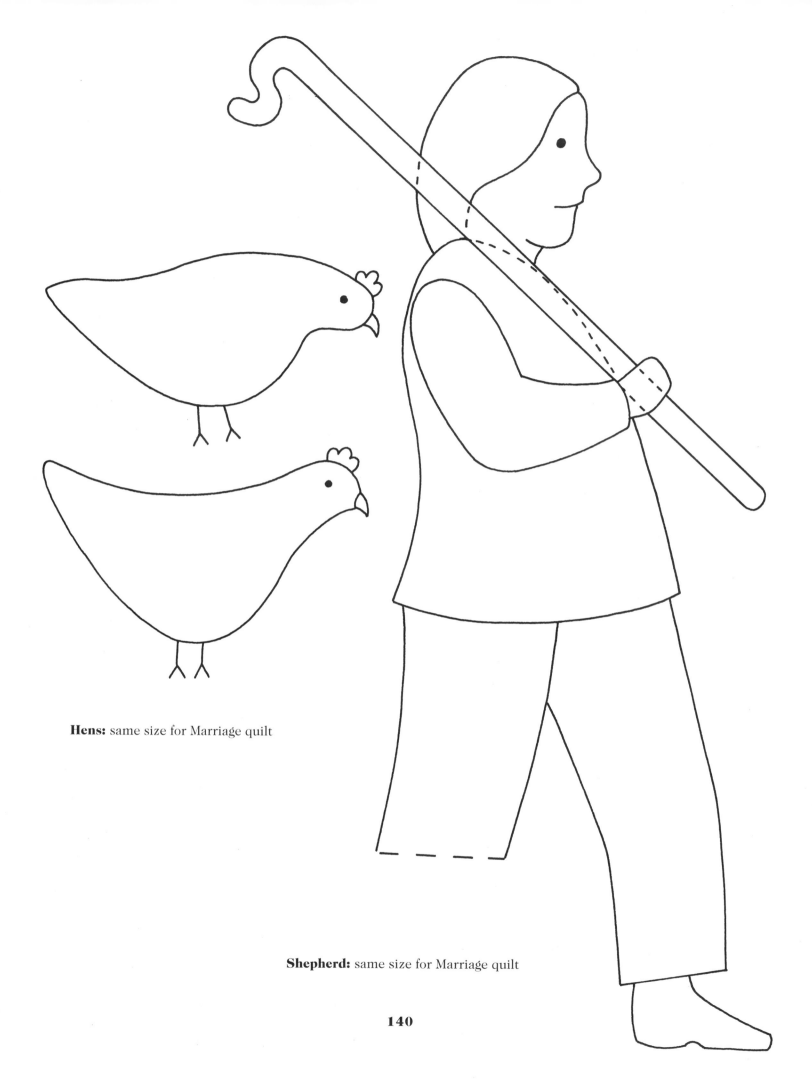

Hens: same size for Marriage quilt

Shepherd: same size for Marriage quilt

140

Heart, stars, maple leaf, circles: same size for Marriage quilt

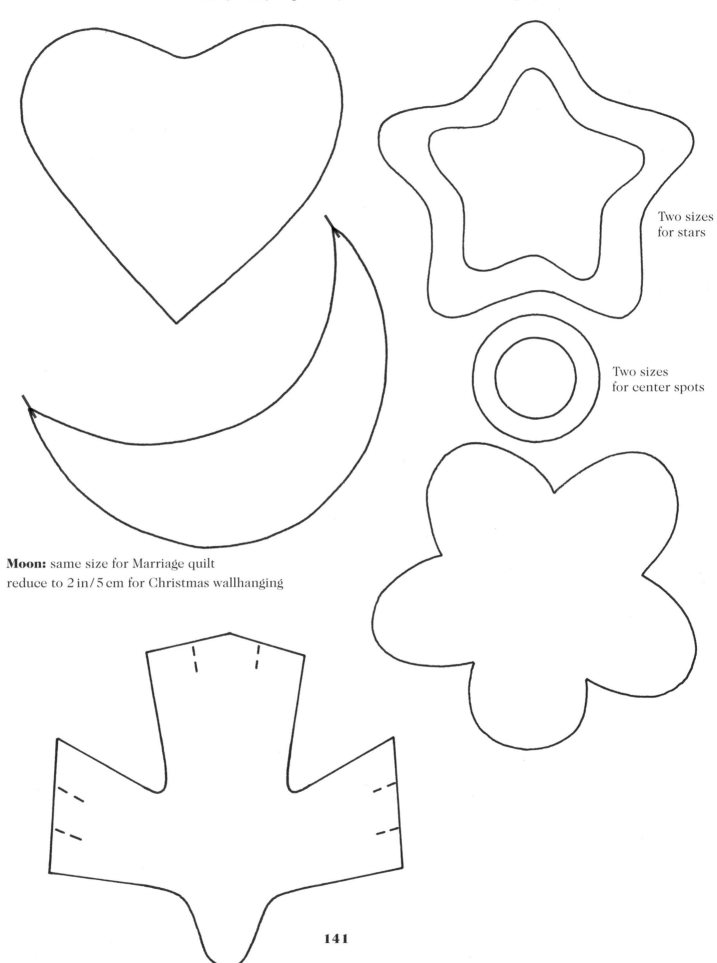

Two sizes
for stars

Two sizes
for center spots

Moon: same size for Marriage quilt
reduce to 2 in / 5 cm for Christmas wallhanging

Milkmaid: same size for Marriage quilt

Use cow from Homestead quilt

Café Curtain:

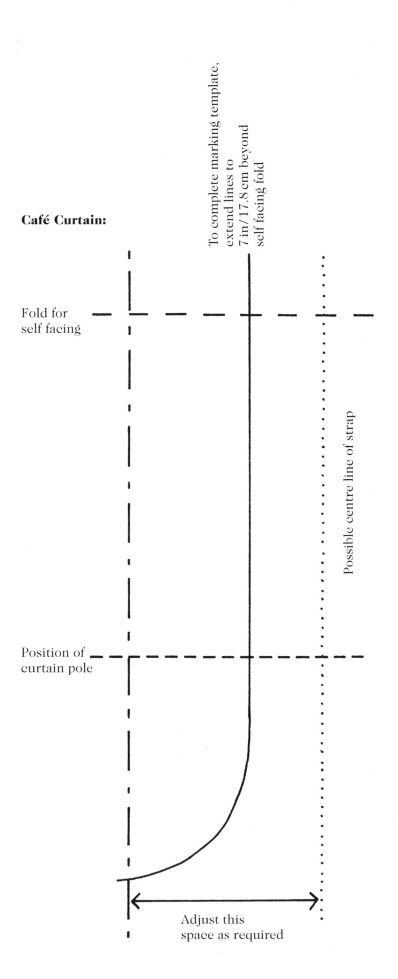

To complete marking template, extend lines to 7 in/17.8 cm beyond self facing fold

Fold for self facing

Position of curtain pole

Possible centre line of strap

Adjust this space as required

Index